FORERUNNERS: IDEAS FIR
FROM THE UNIVERSITY OF

Original e-works to spark n̶e̶w̶ ̶s̶c̶h̶o̶l̶a̶r̶ship

FORERUNNERS: IDEAS FIRST is a thought-in-process series of
breakthrough digital publications. Written between fresh ideas
and finished books, Forerunners draws on scholarly work initiated
in notable blogs, social media, conference plenaries, journal arti-
cles, and the synergy of academic exchange. This is gray literature
publishing: where intense thinking, change, and speculation take
place in scholarship.

Ian Bogost
The Geek's Chihuahua: Living with Apple

Grant Farred
Martin Heidegger Saved My Life

John Hartigan
Aesop's Anthropology: A Multispecies Approach

Reinhold Martin
Mediators: Aesthetics, Politics, and the City

Shannon Mattern
Deep Mapping the Media City

Jussi Parikka
The Anthrobscene

Steven Shaviro
No Speed Limit: Three Essays on Accelerationism

Martin Heidegger Saved My Life

Martin Heidegger Saved My Life

Grant Farred

University of Minnesota Press

MINNEAPOLIS

Published by the University of Minnesota Press
111 Third Avenue South, Suite 290
Minneapolis, MN 55401-2520
http://www.upress.umn.edu

The University of Minnesota is an equal-opportunity educator and
employer.

This book is dedicated to my brother,

Glynn Arthur Farred,

23 October 1963–10 December 1966

You are gone now

just as in my elder youth

my first dreams are gone.

—JOHN SNOW, "Len Bates—Cricketer and Coach"

We do not know what thinking is. But we know when we are not thinking.

—MARTIN HEIDEGGER, *Was heißt Denken?*

Teach thinkers to think,—a needed knowledge in a day of loose and careless logic; and they whose lot is gravest must have the carefulest training to think aright.

—W. E. B. DU BOIS, "Of the Wings of Atalanta"

Contents

Introduction: A Statement of Intent   1

The Question Demands an Answer   7

The Benefits of an Apartheid Education   18

My Debt to Martin Heidegger   25

The Cayuga Heights Dialectic   32

Thoughts Come to Us   37

"Words Are Wellsprings"   44

"Foreign to Its Own Spontaneity"   54

The Only Thing Essential to Thinking
Is Thinking   61

Who Thinks?   76

The Order of the Voice   82

The UnExceptional   87

Acknowledgments   91

Introduction: A Statement of Intent

THE WHITE WOMAN ASKED ME, "Would you like another job?" This was just the question for Guy Fawkes Day.

November 5, Guy Fawkes Day, 2013, was crisp, a bite in the air, like autumn days are supposed to be. As someone who grew up in South Africa, a former British colony, Guy Fawkes Day has a special significance for me. Guy Fawkes Day has historically been celebrated—in Britain and many of its erstwhile colonies, among them Australia, New Zealand, and the seventeenth-century American colonies—with displays of fireworks. (Guy Fawkes Day, or Night, was sometimes known as "Bonfire Night.") The event commemorates the British state's successful quelling of the Gunpowder Plot in 1605, an attempt by English Catholics to assassinate King James I and replace him with a Catholic monarch. One of the plotters, Guy Fawkes—or Guido Fawkes, as he is also sometimes known—was caught beneath the House of Lords with the explosives he was going use to blow up the House. As a cultural figure, Guy Fawkes (and the revolutionary plot) is probably most familiar to Americans as the character at the heart of the movie *V for Vendetta*. (Guy Fawkes is recast as the slightly dubious "freedom fighter" "V" of the movie's title.)

I was on sabbatical for the fall semester of 2013, but I had a meeting with my research assistant on Guy Fawkes Day morning. I wore, as is my custom, a suit and a tie. This is how I dress for the office, a suit and a tie or a jacket and tie. My advisor in graduate school, Andrew Ross, is a proud Scot who dresses with wonderful panache. Andrew once remarked to me when I complimented him on a suit he was wearing, "Only the ruling class can afford to dress down." Ever the anti-Westminster Scot, Andrew was mocking, ever so drolly, the Queen and her tattered gardening cardigans. He is right, of course, the Queen can wear what she wants; she's the Queen, whether she's dressed up in all her royal finery or mucking about the garden in well-worn garb, surrounded by her innumerable corgis. Secure in its position, the ruling class does not have to bother with the niceties of appearance, except for important occasions of state. In truth, taking care with how I dress is a lesson I'd learned growing up in my working-class family in the township of Hanover Park—a sprawling public housing estate located on the "sandy wastes"[1] of the Cape Flats, about half an hour southeast of Cape Town's city center. For the working class, especially the aspirational working class (a category to which most of my family belonged), the appearance of respectability is all. It is a lesson I've learned well.

I came home after the meeting at my office and changed into work clothes—sturdy, water-resistant boots, warm sweat pants, and a sweat shirt, topped by a puff pullover and a wool hat. We live, my wife, Jane, Ezra, our son (who was five years old then), and I, in the Village of Cayuga Heights, the toniest neighborhood in Ithaca, New York. Ithaca is home to Cornell

1. This is a phrase offered to me by the late South African author, a Cape Town native. Rive also used to refer to this region, to which the disenfranchised had been deracinated in the 1960s and 1970s, by apartheid law (the Group Areas Act), as the "windswept Cape Flats."

University, where Jane and I teach. The residence in which Cornell University houses its presidents is located just a quarter mile down the street from us, to give you some idea of the fortunes of the neighborhood. We have colleagues almost immediately to the north, south, and west of us. In Ithaca terms, this is prime real estate and possessed of a bucolic beauty. It is possible to discern, among Ithaca's stately mock-Tudor houses and pretty Cape Cod cottages, the winding streams and the scenic waterfalls, what W. E. B. Du Bois idealizes—writing during his tenure at Atlanta University—as the "low hum of restful life."[2]

Our house is long and sprawling, complete with swimming pool and large grounds (about an acre and a third, not in the least shabby, not even by the standards of Cayuga Heights), and is populated by a fair number of trees. Oak and hickory, mainly, which shed like crazy in the autumn; and the hickory sheds nuts, which attract the deer. I like raking leaves. (On the other hand, I have little affection for the deer who hurdle our four-and-a-half-foot fence with impunity.) Raking leaves is repetitive, almost mechanical labor, but it edifies the soul, or so I tell myself. Good thing I like raking, because it's a never-ending job in the autumn. As soon as you rake the leaves into piles and put them by the side of the road so that the Village of Cayuga Heights Department of Public Works can collect them, there's more. And more . . . I enact the role of a small-time Sisyphus, except the boulder's an endless pile of leaves that I rake up the hill, almost literally, again and again. Sometimes I take the easy option and rake them down the hill.

I'd been raking for about forty minutes on Guy Fawkes Day

2. In this chapter of *The Souls of Black Folk,* written as he overlooks the campus of Atlanta University, where he is then teaching, Du Bois ruminates on the "function of the [Negro] university" in an American South beset by the problem of the "Veil." Du Bois, *The Souls of Black Folk* (New York: Vintage Books/Library of America, 1990), 63.

when a late-model Volvo sedan, white (it had to be white, didn't it?), stopped at the top of the hill, where our house ends, and then reversed about twenty meters to where I was raking. Inside were two distinctly middle-class white people in their late seventies. The elderly Ithaca couple might very well be the prototype of Volvo buyers whom Stanley Fish mocks—condemns, even—in his mischievously titled essay "The Unbearable Ugliness of Volvos"; the white couple in the white Volvo seem like the kind of people who would eschew "ostentation" ("anticommercial virtue") in the name of "safety." Volvos are the perfect car for liberals, Fish argues, because they have no value other than the utilitarian. All over America today (but especially in college towns and other liberal enclaves), the place of Volvos, still reputedly as safe as ever, has been taken by the even more utilitarian, safe (safer than the Volvo), and "ugly" Subarus. The couple in "my" Volvo look like they may very well be the kind of academics (I have no idea if they were active or retired faculty, or perhaps even nothing of the sort) who, as Fish sardonically remarks, one day in the "mid-seventies," "stopped buying ugly Volkswagens and started buying ugly Volvos."

The man, in the passenger seat, was wearing a tweed jacket, while the woman was clad in what looked like a fairly high-end sweater; fine wool, maybe cashmere, if I know my fabrics. She beckoned me over. This act of hers, it was no small thing. Or, this act of hers, small to her, was anything but a routine gesture to me. This act of hers, it immediately put me on my guard.

I am a diasporized black South African. I was raised under the strictures of apartheid. The 1976 student rebellion known as Soweto erupted when I just six months into high school. Growing up under apartheid left its mark on me. In truth, it would have been impossible for it not to because apartheid educated me politically in ways, I have learned in the almost three decades I have lived in the United States, both predictable and unexpected. Because of my political past (which is never really past; one is forever molded by and held within such an experience), I have as a matter of political necessity (apartheid demanded it, if one was to negotiate the unequal terms of South African society with any success) developed a sense for what an encounter that begins with a white person hailing a black person might entail. In such an encounter, as in Deleuze's notion of the statement, "everything . . . is real and all reality is manifestly present." Being summoned, in this way, by a white woman, this was "real": being hailed in this way, this was a real statement of political intent by the white woman. For me, this was a statement loaded with political intent. This encounter, taking place in autumnal, liberal Ithaca, New York, was hauntingly familiar to me. Of course, Ithaca 2013 is not Soweto 1976 or, say, Hanover Park in the midst of the 1980s anti-apartheid insurrection, but being so hailed, this was for me, deep in my bones, nothing other—nothing less—than an apartheid mode of "reality." "Everything" that I knew, even that which I thought I might have forgotten—or repressed—came flooding back, with a deliberate force that took me no time, no time at all, to recognize.

In the instant of my being hailed, apartheid was once again, immediately, "manifestly present." You see, just for a moment, "all that counts is what has been formulated at a given moment." What was being "formulated" for me in Cayuga Heights had been, "at a given moment," "formulated" for me under far more oppressive conditions. These different "formulations," however, concatenated—spoke to each other and, in so doing, spoke to me, reminding me of what "counts" in the act of being beckoned: a black person being beckoned by a white one. All the statements about racial encounters—white people and me, involved in some form of exchange, it was seldom a "conversation" in any recognizable sense—I had "formulated" in a different context, I had to "grudgingly," "inadequately," retrieve.[3] I was once again subject to those "formulations." Unsurprisingly, I had little, if any, difficulty finding access to those statements, and their many evocations, once again.

Every "formulation," however, demands its own response, and so I had to find, in being summoned in Ithaca, my own statement of intent in response to the white woman's question. It was as direct, rhetorically unvarnished and economically grounded a question as one could imagine.

The white woman asked me, "Would you like another job?"

3. I am, of course, generalizing here about the (about my) racial encounter, both in South Africa and in the United States. Many of the critical exchanges I have had, in apartheid and post-apartheid South Africa, have involved white South Africans; likewise in America. Many of my best teachers in South Africa, in high school, in college, and more broadly, speaking culturally, were white, and I retain close links to some, even very close associations (one, in particular) with them; the same applies to my American academic and intellectual experience.

The Question Demands an Answer

> One doesn't think about it before one is forced to think about it.
>
> —JAMES BALDWIN, *The Evidence of Things Not Seen*

IN RESPONSE TO THE WHITE WOMAN'S QUESTION, I would have to answer as a black man in America. It was clear to me, in the moment of being hailed, that I could not rely on the simple act of substitution. I could not make one statement—any of those I produced under apartheid (in 1976; or any I could have offered as a graduate of the mid-1980s insurrection)—stand in for another. Neither would any of those moments in which I had, since arriving in the United States in 1989, rejected the particular violence of American racial inequity suffice now. A new statement, I knew, was necessary.[4]

4. In post-apartheid South Africa, an encounter such as mine would, in South African terms, constitute the very stuff of the comic strip Madam and Eve, produced by Stephen Francis and Rico Schacherl (the strip first ran in July 1992). Madam and Eve mocks the racial reversals that mark contemporary South African life. There is some very deft, dexterous, and revealing verbal sparring between "Madam," the elderly white woman, a remnant of the apartheid mind-set, and the black "Eve," possessed of

Substitution was not possible because, as Deleuze says in his meditation on Michel Foucault as the "new archivist," "statements can be opposed to one another, and placed in hierarchical order." It is crucial to recognize, from the very first, the opposition between the statements. On one hand, there is my statement (that of the diasporic black man), and on the other hand, there is the white woman's, which I take to be the purposive question (which amounts to nothing but a kind of political declarative). The work at hand was to do more than find the statement itself: the statement of the moment, the statement for the moment, the statement that I needed. It was also necessary to find the proper "hierarchical order" of the various statements that I have, over a lifetime, archived—statements that emerge out of the various political encounters where I have had to state, to myself, to those to whom I am close, to those with whom I come into contact as teacher, colleague, friend, my position, to those whom I oppose, state to myself. To produce that statement, I had to decide how things are arranged, in which order they stand, and to do so is always, as we know, a political act. That is why, as Foucault has long since instructed us in *Les Mots et Les Choses,* the order of things matters. That is because something central to our political inclinations is revealed in how we hierarchize things.

As I was being hailed by this white woman in Ithaca, there was, however, also resonating from South Africa another voice. This voice, possessed of a singular authority (there is nothing else that commands us quite like it), reminded me, "These are elderly people. Be polite." This was my mother's voice, calling

a sassy post-apartheid (black) confidence. But their exchanges also offer endearing insights into their "codependent" relationship. Saliently, however, even today, the Cayuga Heights encounter would be recognizable (not entirely beyond the ken) in post-apartheid South Africa.

to me as if I were, just for a moment, back on the streets of the Cape Flats. I was being called back; it was as if I had never left apartheid South Africa. (Indeed, that may be impossible.) From across the Atlantic, making nothing of the intervening decades since my departure to these shores or the eight thousand miles that separate Ithaca from Cape Town, my mother's injunction was clear: "These people are older than you." For my mother, who belongs to the first generation of South Africans raised under apartheid while retaining a British colonial sensibility, age orders how we are in the world; age occupies an elevated place in my mother's social hierarchy, and it comes complete with its own set of demands. "Propriety" does not quite do it justice, but it may convey something of the sentiment that informs my mother's figurative—but audible—intervention. Deference to one's elders, it is how they raise us in the colonies—or, in the settler colonies, that would probably be a more accurate historical description of disenfranchised life in the apartheid state. Propriety is part of my mother's political inheritance, one she bequeathed to her children and grandchildren.

It is because of my history of disenfranchisement that I knew, that I could tell, that I knew in my bones, as they say, what the rhetorical shape, the nature, and, truth be told, I could sense what the content of this encounter between the elderly white woman and the laboring black man would be. It was of no consequence that the black man was laboring in his solitude, on his own property—the "low hum of restful life." I had no doubt that I knew what was about to take place; simultaneously, of course, it was impossible to know. And yet, because I had no doubt, I was prepared, because I was, in James Baldwin's terms, "forced to think about it." But I did not know that I was prepared and what I was prepared for; nor could I know what the effect of my preparation would be. (In his famous *der Spiegel* interview, Martin Heidegger is asked about how he has, in "an exchange with a Buddhist monk," achieved a "completely new method of thinking." Heidegger responds, somewhat disingenuously—but he nevertheless arrests us with his answer—"I know nothing about how this thought has an 'effect.'"[5]) We cannot, of course, know the effect because of its unpredictability—unlike the product, which we can anticipate in advance, there is no knowing what the effect, as Heidegger correctly points out, will yield. I could not anticipate what the effect of my preparation would yield. How apropos Baldwin's remarks on the 1979 Atlanta "child" murders. We think, it seems fair to say, only under the duress—the demand, the expectation—of the moment: "one doesn't think about it before one is forced to think about it." But what a "force" that thinking is; what an "effect" it generates.

Nevertheless, before my preparation—my forced thinking—came to bear on the encounter, I had to acknowledge that there were differences. In racially segregated South Africa, this white woman would have infantilized me in the most offensive but, by apartheid standards, routine way. She would have, in the dominant parlance of apartheid, addressed me, and any other adult black male, as "Boy." (This is classic colonialist discourse. The colonialist denies the Other anything like the courtesies one would afford another fully grown human being, man or woman. In the case of South Africa, the disenfranchised adult was as a matter of course denied the dignity of adulthood. I would have had to answer to, as my father and my grandfather were made to, "Boy."[6] The black South African woman, such as my mother

5. "Only a God Can Save Us" [Nur noch ein Gott kann uns retten], "The *Spiegel* Interview" (1966), http://www.ditext.com/heidegger/interview .html.

6. In the drama *Sizwe Banzi Is Dead,* the authors (Athol Fugard, John Kani, and Winston Ntshona) capture the tenor of this phenomenon. The black man, in the Fugard et al. case, can be desubjectivated not only

or grandmother, would have been similarly rendered, infantilized, as "Girl.") In apartheid South Africa, I would have been expected to accept such an address and answer in its terms; I would have been expected to ask, with forced humility (it never got easier, even with regular practice), when she beckoned me over, "Yes, Madam?" Or, in colloquial Afrikaans, "Ja, Miesies?" or, in formal Afrikaans, "Ja, Mevrou?" depending on the nature of the exchange and the rhetorical shape of the encounter with the white speaker. As a disenfranchised South African, I would have been expected to know not only the transcript, subservience, but also, because white South Africans fell into two language categories, the appropriate language of response. I would have to decide whether the white person addressing me was an English or Afrikaans speaker. Knowing the language of the white person was a lesson taught by the voice; the disenfranchised learned, by listening, carefully, for the linguistic inflections of the white speaker, listening attentively to the intonations so that it became possible to discern the language the voice was "speaking."

This was the everyday political grammar of apartheid, and it

---

through infantilization but also by rendering him generic; the black man is an amorphous black man—one black man is indistinct from, interchangeable with, another. The black man has no individual identity of which to speak, and he certainly does not possess an individuality that white South Africans are bound to respect: "the white man sees [the black man] walk down the street and calls out, 'Hey, John! Come here.'" Athol Fugard, John Kani, and Winston Ntshona, *Sizwe Banzi Is Dead,* in *Statements: Three Plays* (Cape Town: Oxford University Press, 1980), 38. There is, of course, always the pejorative "boy": the "white man says to you, a man, 'Boy, come here.'" Ibid., 43. And, finally, there is the raw face of apartheid. Speaking of his father, "a man full of dignity, a man I respect," the character Buntu has no illusions about the black man's vulnerability in the face of apartheid law because his father can be apprehended as he "walks down the street. White man stops him: 'Come here, kaffir!'" (Ibid.).

was a grammar that had consequences for how different generations of the disenfranchised addressed each other. It produced a distinct, and widely observed, code of conduct, a code that extended, sometimes with severity, to relations between disenfranchised children and adults.

It is because of the ways in which white South Africans, as a matter of course, denigrated disenfranchised adults that no disenfranchised child would dare to address an adult in the child's community by the adult's first name. The proper honorific was always insisted upon. Any other form of address would have been, to understate the matter, frowned upon. For a disenfranchised child to address a disenfranchised adult improperly (without due deference, which is to say, in an informal or casual way) would be regarded as a sign of disrespect or impudence. And such a verbal transgression would have been punished with a stinging verbal rebuke from both the offended adult and the offending child's parents. In fact, the fate that awaited the offending child at home might in all likelihood have been worse.

The strict logic of propriety among the disenfranchised derived from the political reality that there was nothing the disenfranchised adult could do in the face of white South African infantilization but answer to "Boy" or "Girl." Such humiliation was a fact of apartheid life. It was a burden to be borne with resentment. Sometimes this resentment was masked as civility; sometimes it was a burden borne with clenched teeth; sometimes the resentment could not hide a clenched fist; and, yes, there were regular transgressions among the disenfranchised in their treatment of each. It is, however, the larger principle that preoccupies me here, and it certainly applied. For the disenfranchised adult to be addressed in the diminutive by a white child was to be made to know something fundamental about South African racism: apartheid disenfranchisement was, in every way, the condition of being less than. Addressing the disenfranchised adult in the diminutive (making a child of the disenfranchised adult) constituted an absolute negation of disenfranchised adulthood, a refusal of the disenfranchised's right to basic social courtesies. And this is to say nothing of apartheid's legal proscription of equal treatment.

White South Africa's assault on the self-worth of the disenfranchised is what made such behavior by disenfranchised children absolutely *verboten*. This prohibition on disenfranchised children stems from the fact that any white child could, with impunity and as a matter of course, address a disenfranchised adult as "Girl" or by the "Boy's" first name. (Only rarely would a white South African parent instruct his or her children differently or reprimand a child for infantilizing a disenfranchised adult.)[7]

And so the absolute rule that all disenfranchised children must address all disenfranchised adults properly: as "Mr.," "Mrs.," or "Ms." (When I was growing up, it is more likely to have been "Miss." "Ms." belongs to a more contemporary moment.) This code of behavior was inculcated in the home, reinforced on the street by neighbors, burnished to a fine art at school, and given a certain reverence in the church, the mosque, and the temple. (In the disenfranchised community, teachers had a special standing. The parents of schoolchildren would address their children's teachers with the same formality as their children did. It seems that there was always, in the address to the teacher as "Mr.," "Meneer," "Mrs.," "Mevrou," and "Ms.," a special air of respect in attendance.) To address an adult properly, disenfranchised children were taught, was

7. This is not to suggest that there was not, on the part of disenfranchised South Africans, resistance to or anger aimed at this treatment by white South Africans. It is simply to provide a sketch of how the infantilization of the disenfranchised was deeply rooted in the logic of apartheid.

a sign of "good manners"—it was to show that one had respect for one's elders and, what is more, that the children were being raised "properly." Of course, disenfranchised children never had to be taught how to address a white adult; that seemed to come naturally to us. Similarly, and also unsurprisingly, disenfranchised children were taught deference to white children. For some reason, this was a linguistic trick more easily mastered in Afrikaans. One simply resorted to the diminutive honorific: white children could be addressed as "Klein Miesies" ("Little Mrs.") or "Klein baas" ("Little boss," loosely translated). Even if, as was the case in rural areas where economic and social life was arranged around white farms, disenfranchised and white children were playmates. There continue to be remnants of it in post-apartheid society, as J. M. Coetzee's novels *Disgrace* and *Summertime* each, in its own way, reveals.

The Village of Cayuga Heights is, like most faculty enclaves ("ghettoes," in the pejorative) in the United States, predominantly white. For its sins, Cayuga Heights is sometimes, and not unfairly (this is a case of irony well earned), named "Cayuga Whites" by the locals. In my Cayuga Heights, with the white woman driving the Volvo, I was "spared" the diminutive. In America they do things differently.

However, in her summoning me, this white woman returned me to that apartheid "reality" of hierarchies, naming, and, of course, the grammar of infantalization. This white woman seemed to do so without any effort on her part. But, to be fair to her, how could she have known of my "recourse" to the discourse of apartheid? After all, her question arose out of a different, but not entirely distinct, political. (For U.S. blacks, much of life in the United States, North and South, was not that different from life in apartheid South Africa.) I was returned to the apartheid state because, above all else, discernible in her "command"—and it was an imperative, one to which I acceded, for complicated reasons, as we have just seen—was what Jacques Derrida names the "order of the voice."[8] The voice erupts; her voice had erupted, rudely, into the solitariness of my labor; it jolted me out of my contemplations and my physical enjoyment. The power of the voice is that it impels us, sometimes whether we want to or not, to listen. The voice draws us to it. The voice draws unto worlds that are not ours, calls out to us, giving us, as Heidegger says, "food for thought."[9] The voice becomes the stuff of our thinking because the voice makes us think about what it is that calls us. The voice makes a political difficulty of how it is that we are called—how a voice, here or there, from today or long ago, calls out to us. How the voice calls to us, calls other voices, other sounds, other resonances, other inflections to us—every voice has the potential to animate other voices. It seems possible that a single voice, with the smallest calling out, can make every other voice present to us.

The voice in Cayuga Heights, already haunting me just by virtue of hailing me, addressed the question to me. "Would you like another job?" There was no common noun at the end of the question, but it was clearly audible: I knew it as I anticipated I would know it. I was being named "Boy." I was being treated as a "Boy." This woman had clearly discerned, from a cursory glance, not that I like raking leaves for "poetic" purposes but that I would only undertake this task, raking leaves, for remuneration. As such, and for her this would have inevitably followed, I was—inadvertently or not—advertising my availability as cheap labor: as raced cheap labor. It is even possible to suggest that in most instances, given the racial hierarchy that

8. Jacques Derrida, *Of Grammatology,* trans. Gayatri Chavkravorty Spivak (Baltimore: The Johns Hopkins University Press, 1997), 90.

9. Martin Heidegger, *What Is Called Thinking?,* trans. Fred W. Wieck and J. Glenn Gray (New York: Harper and Row, 1968), 22. All further citations to *Was heißt Denken?* are from this translation.

obtains in America, the white woman's logic would have been economically sound—black men performing menial tasks are most assuredly available for hire. It was this particular white woman's misfortune to encounter the exception on Guy Fawkes Day 2013. Right day (every day's the right one for white folks), wrong black man. In disrupting her expectations, it is entirely possible that I constituted for the white woman a variation on Heidegger's "Senegalese negro." In his discussion about the "givenness," the "unitariness," of the lectern, Heidegger introduces a figure of utter disruption. His regular audience, Heidegger says, would see the lectern "in one fell swoop" (as lectern in its full complexity, but also always in its "unitariness") but not so the "Senegalese negro." For this African conjured up by Heidegger, the lectern could be an object of "magic," or it could be a weapon of war—it could provide protection against "arrows" and "stones"; either way, for the "Senegalese negro," the lectern would represent an "instrumental strangeness."[10]

The effect of the white woman's question is that its "instrumentality" (her desire to hire a black man to rake her leaves) was negated by the black man's exceptionality. This exceptionality turned the rhetorical tables on her. The joke was, in this instance, at least, on her. The exception, as Carl Schmitt has long since taught us, releases something "strange" into the exchange, undermining the rhetorical and political authority of the white woman, temporarily reordering Ithaca's racial hierarchy (a racial hierarchy that, as is the liberal tendency, seldom finds public articulation, as such is presumed not to exist). But, as we shall see, the white woman was not the only butt of the joke.

10. *Martin Heidegger, "The Environmental Experience," in The Heidegger Reader,* ed. with an introduction by Günter Figal, trans. Jerome Veith (Bloomington: Indiana University Press, 2009), 34, 35.

For the white bourgeoisie (here we know that Fish is spot-on: driving a utilitarian Volvo or Subaru is merely a political ruse), it seems not to matter very much where they find themselves. "Would you like another job?" is a simple enough inquiry. It means nothing, it is routine. This is the way of the white bourgeoisie. Ask the black laborer directly; no rhetorical courtesy is required. The racialized laborer deserves not a word more than is grammatically necessary. It is not necessary to offer a casual, and certainly not a formal, greeting. There is no need to bother with, "Excuse me, sir"; no, not even a cursory "Hi" is required. Get directly to the point when inquiring from the black man if he wants more work.

For the white woman, the logic is seamless: I have leaves that need to be raked → I see a black man at work, raking leaves → I ask the black man if he wants to rake my leaves → the black man now has, potentially, two jobs raking white people's leaves. As Marx cautioned us about bourgeois illusions, and we will explore this issue in some length later, they may be illusions, but they are necessary illusions—they are illusions necessary for the production of the bourgeoisie. For all those who come into contact with those illusions, the problem is that those illusions have an effect in the world that the bourgeoisie rarely seems to consider.

The Benefits of an Apartheid Education

GROWING UP UNDER AND BEARING WITHIN MYSELF the legacy of apartheid, proved to be—in the Cayuga Heights encounter—"beneficial," in a historically salient way. Apartheid had prepared me well, better than I could ever have imagined, for my Guy Fawkes Day exchange. Well, not exactly like Guy Fawkes Day 2013, but something like it, in general; and to be prepared in general is to be prepared for everything. The effect of that preparation is not only that it lasts a lifetime, that it stays with you longer than you could ever imagine. The effect of that preparation, although I could have never have known this in 1976 or 1987, is that it is immanently translatable. The term *apartheid* may or may not be translatable,[11] but its effects as a form of political pedagogy turned out, in this instance, to be invaluable. (What is more, my encounter in Cayuga Heights is by no means the only time I have found its effects to be politically useful, nor, I am quite sure, will it be the last time I turn to it, or find myself re-turned to it. Guy Fawkes Day 2013 will not be the last time that I find myself faced with apartheid in the United States.)

11. See Jacques Derrida's essay "Racism's Last Word," trans. Peggy Kamuf, *Critical Inquiry* 12 (1985): 290–99, on the question of the "translatability"—the "applicability"—of *apartheid* as a term of political critique.

As a consequence of the political education imposed upon me, I was absolutely prepared for her question. When the white woman asked, "Do you want another job?" I responded, without missing a rhetorical beat, "Only if you can match my Cornell faculty salary." That was all I said and, having made my statement, I turned on my heel. Rather smartly, if I might say so.

No wonder, then, that for Heidegger, "instrumental strangeness" leads to "an event [*Ereignis*]."[12] Saliently, for both Heidegger and the white woman, the event is the effect of scarcity (blackness, or a mode of blackness rarely encountered), strangeness (the Senegalese in the lecture hall; the graduate of apartheid South Africa), and a black man (an entirely disruptive presence). What is stranger? Who is the greater figure of black strangeness? The "Senegalese negro" who wanders into Heidegger's lecture hall, the only black presence in Heidegger's substantial oeuvre, or the black Ivy League professor raking his own leaves? (The "Senegalese negro" is a presence that disturbs Heidegger's essay "The Environmental Experience" because it is, first, so singular and, second, so totally unexpected a presence—whence did Heidegger conjure up the Senegalese? What *Geist*—"spirit"—Derrida would ask, was afoot in Heidegger in that moment? In his critique of the *Geist* of Heidegger's national socialism, Derrida argues that the *Geist* "falls" from "one time into another."[13] We must ask, then, not

12. Heidegger, "Environmental Experience," 37.
13. Jacques Derrida, *Of Spirit: Heidegger and the Question,* trans. Geoffrey Bennington and Rachel Bowlby (Chicago: University of Chicago Press, 1989), 28. Derrida's engagement with Heidegger in *Of Spirit* precipitated a rancorous series of exchanges among Victor Farías (*Heidegger and Nazism*), Phillipe Lacoue-Labarthe (*The Fiction of the Political*), Pierre Bourdieu's postscript in the republication of Michel Foucault's *History of Madness,* and Derrida about Heidegger's "place" in philosophy. (In his 1975 work *The Political Ontology of Martin Heidegger,* Bourdieu's thinking was more in tune with Derrida's more "nuanced" position on Heidegger.)

only how a figure such as the "Senegalese negro" came to Heidegger but also how it is possible to "fall" from Heidegger's time into the time of the "Senegalese negro"—to "fall" from Germany, it matters only a little if it is during the *Reich* or postwar Germany, into colonial West Africa. That is some "fall." Into what time is Heidegger propelling himself? A time he does not know? How does, or could, Heidegger understand the time of the "Senegalese negro"? And why a "Senegalese" and not a Nigerian or Burundian . . . or . . . ? Were there other black figures to whom he did not give voice? What other black figures remain "Unthought" in the Heidegger canon? This question is especially provocative because of the philosophical significance Heidegger attributes to the Unthought: "The more original a thought, the richer its Un-thought becomes. The Unthought is the highest gift [*Geschenk*] a thought can give.")[14]

At some level, then, the joke is on me as much as it is on the white woman. I am the black professor addressed by the white woman as a menial laborer who, in his moment of greatest philosophical need, turns to a thinker historically hostile to "Senegalese negroes" like me. That's intensely paradoxical and, at the very least, a little funny. But again, as we shall see, the white woman and I are not the only ones who are the butt of the joke; and the paradox will intensify.

My first thought, that which came immediately after the statement that I made to the white woman, was an entirely

---

See the chapter "From the Heidegger Affair to the de Man Affair" in Benoît Peters's *Derrida: A Biography,* trans. Andrew Brown (Malden, Mass.: Polity Press, 2013), for a discussion of this controversy.

14. In *Of Spirit,* Derrida pluralizes Heidegger's notion of the "Unthought": "of the thought and the unthoughts or, for I always prefer to say this in the plural, the thoughts and unthoughts of Heidegger" (6).

unlikely one. It struck with a ringing clarity, this thought. This thought presented itself to me, almost pristine and unembellished amid all the tumult in my head. I could hear myself utter this thought, this thought that came after the statement, even though I did not move my lips.

On the other hand, I could not name everything else that was jostling in my head, but it might have been rage and anger, right there alongside a sense of familiarity (and injury too, perhaps) and indignation. Most likely it was accompanied by a vivid flashback—live and in living color, as they say—of apartheid and a profound sense of being psychically assaulted; all of these feelings swirled together, this feeling, rage, say, indistinct from that, indignation. Somewhere in there, too, was a hint of mirth—just the slightest sense of amusement that I had been able to command such a sentence in response the white woman's casual inquiry. Together, these things produced in me a keener understanding than I could have imagined possible of Heidegger's notion of the relationship between thinking and speaking: "only when man speaks, does he think—and not the other way around."[15]

I had spoken, how I had spoken. I had spoken as I had not known I could, or would, speak. In that speaking, about that speaking, Du Bois is right: "they whose lot is gravest must have the carefulest training to think aright." For my own sake, I had had to "think aright." To think, I had to be taught to think when I considered myself—everything about me, my apartheid past, the "low hum" of my raced Ithaca life—to be at stake.

Through my speaking, through the ordering of my voice, I had accomplished, in that moment, thinking.

This accomplishment goes to the core of the thought that

15. Heidegger, *Was heißt Denken?*, 16.

followed, immediately, my speaking. Let me state it: "Thank God for Martin Heidegger." This was quickly followed by, "Thank God for *Was heißt Denken?*" There was barely a breath in between my response and my giving thanks: I spoke in the direction of Martin Heidegger because Martin Heidegger had saved my life. (Ironically, Heidegger had saved my life through what he bemoans, in the *der Spiegel* interview, as his "least read" book; how Heidegger determined the lowly status of *Was heißt Denken?* is unclear.) Not only Heidegger, of course, but also apartheid (how the ironies compound) and my mother (whose resonating, historic voice issued a caution); mainly, however, it was Heidegger I thanked.

For years now I have been reading Martin Heidegger, again and again, teaching him, writing about Heidegger, using Heidegger to take up other questions, other authors—seemingly unable to get too far away from Heidegger. And always with Heidegger scholar Thomas Sheehan's caution in mind about my capacity to think Heidegger. "When it comes to Heidegger," Sheehan says, borrowing an analogy from what is said about Hegel, "there are no experts, only varying degrees of ignorance."[16] (In light of the scandal that is the publication of the *Schwartze Hefte*—the *Black Notebooks*—it also seems advisable to follow David Farrell Krell's caution when we, now, read Heidegger: "It is clearly a matter of reading as much as one can and worrying ceaselessly about the blindness that accompanies insight.")[17] Struggling with Heidegger, from *Sein und Zeit* to the *Schwartze Hefte,* is what one does with Heidegger so as to decrease the "degree of ignorance" and—in that struggle, as it has always been, in one way or another—to remind oneself always about the brilliance of Heidegger's "blindness."

16. Thomas Sheehan, *Making Sense of Heidegger: A Paradigm Shift* (New York: Roman and Littlefield, 2015), xix.

About that there can be no question. However, Sheehan confesses his "ignorance" (although there are few scholars of Heidegger who know more about Heidegger than Sheehan and, of course, Krell), invites critique, to "show a clearer way beyond" Heidegger.[18]

17. David Farrell Krell, *Ecstasy, Catastrophe: Heidegger from "Being and Time" to the "Black Notebooks"* (Albany: State University of New York Press, 2015), 218.

18. Sheehan, *Making Sense of Heidegger,* xix.

My Debt to Martin Heidegger

FOR MY PART, in that moment, I understood one thing above all else: that I owed my response to Martin Heidegger. My debt to Heidegger is the debt of the reader of Heidegger. My debt is to Heidegger as a thinker who, in my engagement with him, always insists upon the thinking of thinking even as I know that he turned his thinking only rarely—once, publicly—to me, and then in a way that was hardly flattering; and even before the publication of the *Schwartze Hefte,* Heidegger's anti-Semitism was well known;[19] take his repeated attacks on the *Judentum* (or *Weltjudentum*) for their *Weltlosigkeit*—their world-"poorness." "The Jew lacks world and earth," in Krell's rendering.[20] All this, and still the paradox, I remind myself again and again, retains its force and is striking: the philosopher who makes me think could only, in his day, at the height of his philosophical powers, conjure someone like me as a "Senegalese negro." And yet Krell, while rebuking Heidegger for the signal failure of the

19. For example, in his work *Heidegger, l'introduction du nazisme dans la philosophie* [Heidegger: The introduction of Nazism into philosophy] (Frankfurt am Main, 2005), Emmanuel Faye strongly recommends that Heidegger's writing be cataloged not under "Philosophy" but under the "History of Nazism."

20. Krell, *Ecstasy, Catastrophe,* 171.

Schwartze Hefte (a stinging critique: "For one whose pride was *thinking,* the *Black Notebooks* of the 1930s and early 1940s represent a tragic collapse"), refuses to let anyone, himself least of all, off the hook—"racism did not first arise during the 1930s in Germany . . . carcinogens are found in so many peoples, in so many places, at so many times."[21] Indeed, not all "carcinogens" are the same, nor do they have the same effects in the world, but they are, "carcinogens," to be found in apartheid South Africa (officially, from 1948 to 1990), in liberal Ithaca, New York (2013), in . . . In the second part of *Ecstasy, Catastrophe,* Krell is doing nothing other than "thinking" about Heidegger's failure to think; Krell castigates Heidegger for failing himself and "descending" into that form of discourse Heidegger most despised: polemic.

To be troubled by Heidegger, then, is never an uncomplicated matter. I am troubled by Heidegger, by the knowledge that the "Senegalese negro" is unthought by a thinker who enjoins me, insofar as it is possible, to leave nothing "unthought." Unlike Krell, I do not "worry ceaselessly," but I can understand his proclivity. There is every reason for me to be concerned about Heidegger and how often I turn to his work. Like Krell, I never lose sight of what draws me to Heidegger: the central provocation of his work—to think. In *De l'esprit (Of Spirit: Heidegger and the Question),* Derrida thinks with Heidegger to excavate the "carcinogens" in Heidegger's thinking.

So for that moment, I neither sought an explanation (from Heidegger? from myself?) about the "Senegalese negro," nor did I seek, as Sheehan enjoins us to, a "way beyond." It was enough to be thinking. In his biography of Heidegger, *Between Good and Evil,* Rüdiger Safranski argues that Heidegger "criticizes any philosophy that professes to have its beginnings in

21. Ibid., 215, 218.

thought."[22] According to Safranski, for Heidegger, philosophy "begins with a mood, with astonishment, fear, worry, curiosity, jubilation."[23] *Between Good and Evil* is perhaps the best biography of Heidegger, and Safranski makes a good case for how to approach Heidegger's philosophy. However, what I take from Heidegger seems to contradict Safranski because my engagement with Heidegger always "begins in thought." This may very well be my shortcoming, or it may be that every time I turn to Heidegger, there it is, the challenge to think. It is constitutively, "definitively" present in *Was heißt Denken?*; it is at the core of *Der Satz vom Grund (The Principle of Reason)*; it girds his essay "The Principle of Identity"; it guides his work in "Bauen, Wohnen, Denken"; and so on.

Heidegger: on thinking. Heidegger: teaching himself, and us, to think. Heidegger provokes Derrida to turn his attention, and the latter does so with wit and a marvelous ambivalence in *De l'esprit,* to the *"Geist, geistig, geistlich"*[24] that guides Heidegger's thinking. What I am naming Derrida's ambivalence reaches its apogee in his most searching (because it is, in truth, unanswerable, as such) question. If the "thought of race *(Rassengedanke)* is interpreted in metaphysical and not biological terms," "is a metaphysics of race more or less serious than a naturalism or a biologism of race?"[25] Heidegger, it is possible to say, provides— through his commitment, and failure, to thinking—a ready-to-hand answer to this, the most probing of Derrida's inquiries. In Heidegger's case, the more "original" is a thinker, the more terrifying is the "gift" *(Geschenk)* of his Unthought (or the articulation of the Unthought as a polemic). The more "original" a

22. Rüdiger Safranski, *Between Good and Evil,* trans. Ewald Osers (Cambridge, Mass.: Harvard University Press, 2002), 1.

23. Ibid.

24. Derrida, *Of Spirit,* 1.

25. Ibid., 74.

thinker is, and there can be no doubt that Heidegger is such a thinker, the more urgent is the need to confront that thinker's Unthought. Few of Heidegger's critics understand this as well as Derrida. Heidegger, Derrida says, "leaves us with the *injunction* to think what he does not think."[26] We must think precisely what Heidegger does not; in this way, Heidegger makes, say, *Rassengedanke,* a project for thinking. It is, then, because of Heidegger's not thinking, to phrase the matter provocatively, that we are drawn into thinking what matters to us. Following Derrida's "injunction," *Rassengedanke,* in the Reich, in apartheid South Africa, in Ithaca, sets up a *Gespräch,* a conversation in which each racial/racist episteme must be accounted for, between the "original" *Denker* and the reader of that *Denker.* Here Krell's caution seems especially well warranted—and of a piece with Derrida's opening up of Heidegger. In reading Heidegger, one must "worry ceaselessly," never more so than when Heidegger calls one to think.

Nevertheless, it is because of Heidegger's insistent call to thinking that he occupies the singular place he does in this essay. Apartheid may very well have prepared me for my encounter with the white woman, but it was "clear" to me was that it was Heidegger who had saved me. And this is why Heidegger saved me. Martin Heidegger poses for me, again and again, the question of thinking: "We do not know what thinking is." In that philosophical assertion, the question that is decidedly not a question, resides the force of *Was heißt Denken?* What other philosopher makes such an assertion?[27]

26. As quoted in Peeters, *Derrida: A Biography,* 384, emphasis original.
27. In response to this question, as much as anywhere else in this essay, Descartes's famous postulation on thinking is audible: "cogito ergo sum" (/ˈkoʊɡɪtoʊ ˈɜrɡoʊ ˈsʊm/, also /ˈkɒɡɪtoʊ/, /ˈsʌm/; classical Latin: [ˈkoːɡitoː ˈɛrɡoː ˈsʊm]—"I think, therefore I am," or, what is sometimes presented as a closer approximation, "I am thinking, therefore I exist."

In my encounter with the white woman, I had the grammar of apartheid to hand. However, the logic of apartheid was an object lesson in what not to say (follow the racist script). This apartheid injunction is biopolitically valuable in itself, of course, but it was not quite what was needed in Cayuga Heights. Martin Heidegger saved me because it is he who makes me, made me, think about what to say before I was called upon to say it—before I was "forced to think about it." I would not have been, without Heidegger, bereft of a response, but it would not have been the work of thinking—it would not have been in any sense worthy of the work on *thinking* Heidegger has done.

That is the critical distinction that I must acknowledge. There is a crucial difference between the response produced

---

According to Descartes, there is first thinking, followed by existence; insofar as there is existence, there is (already, a priori) thinking. Thinking qua thinking, the "thingness" of thinking itself, however, is not a project that Descartes pursues. (In *Sein und Zeit,* Heidegger, much as he acknowledges Descartes's role in the history of metaphysics, offers a critique of Cartesianism.) However, given the historic resonance of "cogito ergo sum," it is possible to identify Descartes as the philosopher who provides something like the *Grund* for *Was heißt Denken?* and the figure who is most evocatively present in Heidegger's notion of thinking. In his critique of Immanuel Kant, *Kant and the Problem of Metaphysics,* we see this clearly: "Time and 'I think' are no longer opposed to one another as unlike and incompatible; they are the same"—Heidegger attributes this "gathering" together of the Cartesian "coupling" to Kant's "transcendental interpretation." Heidegger, *Kant and the Problem of Metaphysics,* trans. Thomas Langan (Bloomington: University of Indiana Press, 1962), 197. It is worth noting here that Kant is key for Heidegger's work on thinking. In texts such as his essay "What Is Enlightenment?" (a critique of the state and religious institutions and a call for individuals to be allowed to make their own determinations; to "think for themselves"), *Critique of Pure Reason* (an argument for the limit of reason) and *Metaphysics of Morals* (how we can be governed by reason), thinking is very much a part of the work Kant undertakes.

by thinking and the response devoid of it, what Heidegger identifies as the "polemic"—"Any kind of polemic fails from the outset to assume the attitude of thinking."[28] (Refusing polemic is, in Krell's terms, precisely the test that Heidegger fails in *Schwartze Hefte*: "throughout the *Black Notebooks* is the increasingly violent polemic against everyone and everything, a polemic that suffocates every conceivable effort at thinking."[29]) To "assume the attitude of thinking," the "polemic" must be eschewed because it amounts to nothing but the failure of thinking. Thinking becomes, in the Cayuga Heights encounter, the response par excellence to the Unthought[30] question of the white woman. "Would you like another job?" is the question that is without thinking; it lacks thinking because, in this situation, the white woman need only adhere to the terms of the dominant racial discourse. Hers is a rote inquiry, rooted in a history shaped by the power of whiteness, indifferent to any "injunction," and for precisely that reason, it bears no relation to thinking.

The only proper political response to the question that is presented without thinking, the question that is rooted in an objectionable politics, is to "speak" thinking. It is to think before, long before, you are called upon to speak.

28. Heidegger, *Was heißt Denken?,* 13.
29. Krell, *Ecstasy, Catastrophe,* 159.
30. In response to Heidegger's "Unthought" in *Was heißt Denken?,* Derrida takes up this notion in *Of Spirit,* and Foucault offers an illuminating discussion on it in "Man and His Doubles," a chapter in *Le Mot et les choses,* 303–43 (New York: Vintage Books, 1973).

The Cayuga Heights Dialectic

THE CAYUGA HEIGHTS ENCOUNTER is grounded in an a priori dialectic. Without properly knowing it (it is impossible to know it in advance, however prepared one is), my fidelity to thinking (Heidegger) is what allowed for my response; and my rejection of not-thinking is located not only in my response to the woman's question but in reminding myself that what is truly unacceptable is my not thinking about what needed to be said. The latter is clearly a prospect I dread. If I had not offered the statement—"Only if you can match my Cornell faculty salary"—I did, it would have meant that I had not learned to think—"We must learn thinking"—and in that encounter, nothing could have been, for me, more politically irresponsible than not thinking.[31] The unthinking response to the routine (racist?) question can only be described as a failure—or a provocation—of Heideggerian (and Derridean as well as Foucauldian, dare one say?) proportions. To not think is to be, in Heidegger's terms, "poor in thought"—the rote question has value only insofar as it provokes the turn to thinking the "Unthought" of the question. (This provokes its own particular line of inquiry, one entirely distinct from Derrida's "injunction." We know that Heidegger

31. Heidegger, *Was heißt Denken?*, 17.

can make us think about what he does not think, but the question of record is, can not-thinking make us think? The answer can be found in another question, which is little other than a declarative: Is there anything else that is more likely to make us think than to be faced with not-thinking?) The black man's Unthought: Heidegger's is an objectionable politics; he owes his coming to thinking to Heidegger (insofar as the thinking is, already before itself, the "injunction" he takes as his own). If the black man "gives up" Heidegger on the grounds of the German philosopher's politics, what kind of thinking has he learned? If he remains faithful to the Heideggerian injunction to always learn thinking, what kind of *Rassengedanke* can he undertake? As always with Heidegger, to borrow Krell's *De l'esprit* rendering of Heidegger, "there are traps on all sides."[32] Faced with these "traps," there is nothing to do but think.

This is how Martin Heidegger saved me: first, he made me think about thinking—about learning to think, about living with his repeated challenge that "most thought-provoking for our thought-provoking age is that we are still not thinking"—and second, he translated the question about what I would have said to the white woman if I had not been thinking, in the terms of *Was heißt Denken?*, into a matter for thinking.

This act of translation is the only guarantee I have (a guarantee that is itself not guaranteed, of course) that I am thinking about thinking. I was thinking about what I did not say so that my thinking—about what was left out, omitted, not said, but reflected upon repeatedly afterward—was, in the most productive sense, the result of my being haunted by an absence. The negative force of thinking, one is almost tempted to name it, because, on one hand, it did not matter what I did not say; on the other, that is precisely what must be subjected to thinking,

32. Krell, *Ecstasy, Catastrophe,* 182.

the consequence of the "thoughtful questioning" addressed to the absence that is not an absence but the presence of a haunting.[33]

Why did I not say what I did not say? Why did I not say what I could have said and would, in narrow political terms, have been fully justified in saying? This leads to the question, "Why Heidegger?" to which we will return in a form expanded to address other proper names, names whose nonuse will trouble my turn to Heidegger, which is of course encapsulated in the title of this essay, "Martin Heidegger Saved My Life." (*Rassengedanke*, as we shall see, of a different order—an order that turns on the names of figures who take race as their point of political entrée.) This questioning, which might be more or less "thoughtful," will lead back, in the most provocative way, to *the* question, "Why not Heidegger?" which is itself a declarative negation—a clear commitment to thinking about thinking—of the first question (and the Unthought that constitutes it).

Something of that ambivalence, the tug and pull between questions, as it were, was present in that single moment when the only sentence I could construct was "Thank God for Martin Heidegger," when that was the thought that dominated my being.

I know that it is strange, but I did not, until I undertook to write this essay, ask, How could have I have produced, in that moment, as an answer to the white woman's question, the response that I did? How did my speaking come to bear on my thinking? How did it come to bear thinking in just this form and not any other?[34] Attribution was not an issue in the

33. Heidegger, *Was heißt Denken?*, 169.

34. In this regard, Reiner Schürmann's critique of *Sein und Zeit* is instructive and insightful: "*Being and Time* analyzes the structure that makes such a pre-understanding of the regions of being possible. That pre-understanding is no longer a cognitive one. The first prejudice, the system-

moment when I stated my thoughts as I did, which is clearly a problem. It is explicable that attribution was not the first (or second or . . .) order of business in the wake of my response, because preoccupation with the encounter is what took precedence, but it is still a problem, hence the turn to thinking (why was attribution not a problem?) after thinking (my response, indebted to Heidegger). Attribution is always, now, as it surely was then, in the moment of articulation, itself a matter of no small consequence.

You see, from the time I was a boy growing up in Cape Town, I must have been practicing, turning words over in my head, arranging, rearranging, the order of the words, in anticipation of just such an encounter. The words that seem to have come out of my mouth, the words were spoken exactly as they should have. I could not have known that it would come to me where it did, in Ithaca, New York, but I must have been constructing that sentence in my head for all of my life. It came to me, that sentence, fully formed, full of thought, formed in and by thought.

However, I did not construct that sentence by myself, so attribution is at the heart of everything. This we can easily glean from the intensity of the attribution: "Thank God for Martin Heidegger," a colloquial, everyday phrase made to do extraordinary work (extraordinary philosophical work, Safranski might say) in, and because of, the encounter. There is, as is always true, something adversarial in attribution—otherwise I would not struggle with it so. To acknowledge Martin Heidegger it is

---

atic precedence of knowing over all other activities, is thereby broken." Schürmann, *Heidegger: On Being and Acting: From Principles to Acting* (Bloomington: Indiana University Press, 1990), 301. In that Ithaca moment, I take this to mean that it is not necessary "at all" that I "know" where my articulation—the thought response to the rote question—comes from because the "first prejudice" of "systematic precedence" has been "broken."

clearly a difficulty for me, and with good political reason (as I have shown); and yet it is not. In choosing "this" (thinker) rather than "that" (other thinker, or thinkers), that is to know firsthand that there is something of substance at stake in that choice, in the figure to whom we attribute our thinking.[35]

35. The notion of "adversarial" is taken from Heidegger's "The Thinker as Poet": "If in thinking there were already / adversaries and not mere / opponents, then thinking's case / would be more auspicious." Martin Heidegger, "The Thinker as Poet," in *Poetry, Language, Thought,* trans. Alfred Hofstadter (New York: Harper and Row, 2001), 5.

Thoughts Come to Us

> We never come to thoughts. They come to us.
> —MARTIN HEIDEGGER, "The Thinker as Poet."

THOUGHTS COME TO US. That bears thinking about. Our thoughts must, themselves, apprehend us in our thinking—"In thinking all things / become solitary and slow"—as we seek to trace our thinking.[36] In thinking we stand, by ourselves, gathered into the thought of others, gathered by the thought of others, gathering others into our thinking. All the while our thoughts seek to gather others unto us. To understand how thoughts come to us is, as Heidegger knows, a "slow" but not necessarily deliberate process—or, deliberative, it is certainly a process that cannot be charted teleologically.

In apprehending myself, I now know that I had philosophical help that can be traced to nowhere but Heidegger because, in his terms, this thought—this thought that had spared me, saved me—had been "given" to me from "elsewhere"; from Heidegger. There can be no disputing this "arrival" of the thought that had come to me, ordered, as it were, exactly as I needed it. The thought had come to me because I had long since been

36. Heidegger, *"Thinker as Poet,"* 9.

called to thinking: I had, I must have been, thinking this a priori, I must have sought to learn this thought, to learn to think in this way and not any other. Before I thought this I was thinking this so that I was, not to put too fine a point on it, ready to "receive" the thought; I was prepared for the thought to come to me. I had been thinking this because I had long been living in this mode of "solitude" (preoccupied in my work with Heidegger and thinking); as Heidegger says, it is "only from solitude that all thinking, in a hidden mode, speaks to the thinking that comes after or went before."[37] My "speaking"—the response produced by thought; the thoughtful response—to the white woman marks a moment of "solitude," but more importantly, it reveals itself as that "hidden mode" that is the direct outcome of the thinking that came "after or went before." No act of speaking as thinking stands by itself. Every act of thinking always bears within itself traces of every other thinking, every other act of learning to think, every other instance of living—how important this is—with the *Geschenk* that is the Unthought.

But how is it that we are called to think? Heidegger takes up this issue through the question, "What calls for thinking on our part?" It "could of course," he says, "intend no more than 'What does the term "thinking" signify to us?' But the question, asked properly, 'What calls for thinking on our part?,' means something else. . . . It means: What is it that directs us into thought and gives us directives for thinking?"[38] What is it that calls us to thinking? This is a question to which Heidegger returns again and again, a question that seems to come up every time thinking is learned, is undertaken, or presents itself as a philosophical

37. Heidegger, *Was heißt Denken?*, 169.
38. Martin Heidegger, *Basic Writings*, ed. David Farrell Krell (London: HarperPerennial, 2008), 384.

difficulty. In so doing, Heidegger constructs an unbreakable bond—a singularity of intellectual project—between philosophy and thinking: "only philosophy thinks" is how he asserts it.[39]

It is only possible to undo racism (*Rassengedanke*) at the level of language—to destroy the grounds on which it operates, if only for a moment, presuming, of course, that such a destruction can be achieved (we are always in the business of envisaging the end of racism)—if you think about why it is you think about racism. What is it that "directs us into thought and gives us directives for thinking?" Of this we can be sure: it is entirely likely that it is racism—or any form of discrimination or violence—that calls us (first) to (this, and not any other, or this in addition to one or several others) thinking, but we are called to think before we are called to think about racism. Thinking comes before everything else (the first-ness of "cogito ergo sum," as it were; or, living, either happily or in discomfiture, with the ghost of Descartes). Thinking is the condition that makes everything else possible. Thinking racism "follows" thinking. (Even, as is clear from the trajectory I delineate, thinking—recognizing how Heidegger locates thinking in "philosophy"—race and racism is always only a short step behind my thinking "philosophy." My thinking always has, as it

39. In "response" to Heidegger's declarative, Derrida asks this question: "What is expected of the philosopher? That he be the functionary of the fundamental. These misunderstandings, more full of life today than ever, are sustained, notes Heidegger (and who will argue with him?), by teachers of philosophy." Derrida, *Of Spirit,* 42. For their part, in What Is Philosophy?, Gilles Deleuze and Félix Guattari define it as the "art of forming, inventing, and fabricating concepts" (they occasionally capitalize "Concept"). Deleuze and Guattari, *What Is Philosophy?,* trans. Hugh Tomlinson and Graham Burchell (New York: Columbia University Press, 1994), 2. Here Heidegger's privileging of thinking throws the "creation of the concept" into relief because neither creation nor the concept is possible without, a priori, thinking.

were, a "subject" to hand; there is always a "subject" to which my thinking is attuned.[40]) In this regard, thinking (A) racism (B) must be understood as a mode that is at once sequential (B comes after A) and entangled (B is already present in A), producing thinking as a praxis that turns on thinking but can be put to distinct, specific purposes. It is only possible to think racism if—after—thinking has been undertaken. Thinking racism— or misogyny or anticolonialism, xenophobia or homophobia— comes only after we have accepted the call to think about how it is we think. In trying to establish the grounds of thinking and then to understand how it is we "apply," "direct," or "instrumentalize" our thinking, we know that the "matter of thinking is confounding."[41] Indeed, for the black man raised under apartheid to turn first to thinking (to turn first to Heidegger; to always live under the sign of the Heideggerian injunction "to think") is "confounding"—and, as previously acknowledged, a paradox. However, such a representation only beggars political belief if one does not assign thinking precedence, that is, if thinking is uncoupled from *Rassengedanke* (from thinking race), when thinking and thinking racism are set in an artificial and needless opposition to each other.

Accepting the call to think is the first "directive" of thinking. To think, there must be fidelity to abstraction (to, in Derrida's phrase, accept the role of "functionary of the fundamental"), however "confounding" it may be.[42] There must be fidelity to thinking thinking in and on its own terms, terms we can never fully know but are continually striving to achieve; we

40. A "subject," as such, that always bears on the Satrean "object." In and because of every intersubjective encounter, Sartre argues in *L'Être et le néant: Essai d'ontologie phénoménologique (Being and Nothingness)* that there is the possibility of turning the "subject" into an "object."

41. Heidegger, *Was heißt Denken?*, 13.

42. Derrida, *Of Spirit*, 42.

are constantly trying to teach ourselves to think. Again, "We do not know what thinking is," but to think, it is imperative to commit, again and again, to thinking so that it becomes possible to learn thinking. To think the encounter or the event *(Ereignis),* or what I have named elsewhere the Situation,[43] to think in the encounter, thinking as such must have already preceded everything and must already be present. As such, thinking must, because of our inclining toward thought, make its presence known.

The key word in my phrasing, "Only if you can match my Cornell faculty salary," is not, as might be imagined, "Cornell." It is tempting, and logical (in the imaginary that is Ithaca, where all psychic and no small amount of economic life of the community turns on the university, as is true of many college towns), to nominate "Cornell" as the pivotal term in my response. (My office at Cornell University's Africana Center sits just three minutes southwest of where the encounter took place.) But "Cornell" is not the crucial term. Neither is it "salary," already in itself a class critique that the white woman could not have expected. In this regard, "Only if you can match my Cornell faculty salary" stands as a conditional: it depends on whether you (the white woman) can meet my (the black man's) standards. This is a further statement of intent glossed as an invitation—a throwaway line containing within it a mocking challenge, feel free to match my salary—that is also an outright dismissal: the black man will work for you if you can "match" his salary. Who pays the menial worker a professorial salary? It is, of course, in a shrinking professoriate (with adjunct labor increasing and the number of tenure track jobs diminishing—a condition that has its own iterations in the United States but is intensified in

43. See Grant Farred, *In Motion, At Rest: The Event of the Athletic Body* (Minneapolis: University of Minnesota Press, 2014).

other parts of the globe), no small matter to be a full professor at an elite American institution.

In the case of my encounter, the key "word" is, as Heidegger writes, "related to thought, memory and thanks."[44] The key word in the encounter is "faculty." The word *faculty* is a powerful term of negation that emerges from what can only be identified as racist preconceptions. The black man whom the white woman addresses as a menial laborer is, in her psychic imaginary of Ithaca, inconceivable: he is a professor. At the very least, he is as well educated as she is. The word *faculty* is also deeply rooted in both the white woman's and the black man's "memory." Her "memory" is in no way attuned to the possibility of laboring black men as Ivy League faculty, a matter that will be explored a little more shortly. For the black man, the "memory" of apartheid comes flooding back—the "Boy" cannot be a professor. The United States recalibrates the memory of racism, it does not eradicate it; the United States keeps, as it were, memory alive; it gives the memory of race and racism a new and sustainable life. And, last though by no means least, the word bespeaks a philosophical gratitude, inscribed from (almost) the very beginning of this thinking—"Thank God for Martin Heidegger"—that has its roots in the faculty of the black man's thinking.

All of which adds a certain philosophical trajectory to what is a clear statement of intent. This sentence traces itself "back" to something other than the black man's response; it arches (it aches) in the direction of another phrasing. This statement does not stand by itself; it never did. Nevertheless, it retains its distinctness, its integrity, if you will. In the word *faculty* is the speaking of a deliberate repudiation of the white woman: this black man is a worker whom you cannot afford. The structure

44. Heidegger, *Was heißt Denken?*, 163.

of the sentence is such that the black can reprimand (mock? ridicule?), in the most polite way, the white woman by articulating an impossible availability. Nevertheless, the black worker remains, as we will see (class position or no), an object for misapprehension: how the black man (at work) is apprehended does not depend on his attire. Although, it must be said, in certain situations, what you wear can insulate you from an inquiry as unthinking—as brazen—as this. On the campus of Cornell University itself (or on the campus of any other institution, Duke University, Williams College, the University of Michigan), I have never encountered anything remotely similar to what I did on my own property.

"Words Are Wellsprings"

> Words are wellsprings that are found and dug up
> in the telling, wellsprings that must be found and
> dug up again and again, that easily cave in, but that
> at times also well up when least expected.
> —MARTIN HEIDEGGER, *Was heißt Denken?*

"FACULTY," THEN, IS THE WORD OF RECORD. What mattered
was the status "faculty" accorded me because it named the
black worker a professor, a standing entirely incommensu-
rate with the white woman's illusion. The black man raking
leaves cannot be reconciled with an Ivy League professor, in
"her" community, right here in "Cayuga Whites." Immediately,
because of that response, her line of inquiry is revealed as a
transgression. The "voice" of the Other, Derrida might say,
functions as a call to "conscience" if "conscience" (à la *Ham-
let*) is figured as the irruption of thinking that is produced by
the offense. Whether the call to conscience is heard or not, it
is almost impossible (for the offending party, the white woman,
in this case) to do anything but retreat when one is so brutally
exposed. Worst of all, when you have not in the least expected
the Other's response; when, to phrase it as a matter of political asymmetry, you have had no preparation for the riposte. All

that the white woman can do, then, is drive off in her Volvo. The other option, of which the white woman shows herself incapable, is that of thinking: to speak (to think), in the face of the response, to the content—the politics, we could easily say—of the question that the white woman posed; to speak to the manner—the tone—in which the white woman posed the question; and, most importantly, to think that thought—the question (which here resembles Derrida's "injunction")—back to its very first incarnation, to its Unthought. If the Other's response begins under the condition of apartheid, where did the white woman's question find its earliest composition? What made her question? What is it that did not make of the question she posed, before all else, a question?

Here Heidegger's "words" function in two ways. First, the words offered, thought, by the black man belongs to both the category of retrieval—words that are "found and dug up again and again"—and the unexpected. The latter are the kinds of words that "well up when least expected," and it is their timing—their sense of moment—that makes them philosophically and politically invaluable. Second, these are the words that, much as they belong to the same wellspring of (everyday) words, derive their significance from their refusal to "cave in"—to submit—to the discursive formation envisaged by the white woman. These are words that, at once, enact the power of the black man and lay the white woman linguistically to waste. These are not, as such, the words of resistance (tempting as it is to represent them as such); they are, rather, words that demonstrate the power of thinking to make the encounter about nothing but thinking; it marks, reductively phrased, the triumph of thinking over nonthinking, of thinking over those beings who resist the imperative of the Heideggerian Unthought. The black man's professional reality, Ivy League professor, is the "trap" that the white woman could not anticipate.

Because the white woman was unable to change her modality from not thinking to thinking, she could not—she might not have been predisposed to do so, anyway—apprehend the black man's response as a question, as the question of thinking. Having followed up her rote inquiry with the refusal to think, all that the white woman could do was drive away, hurriedly. Was that unceremonious departure an admission of not-thinking? Of shame? Embarrassment? Shock, absolute shock, at the black man's response? An explicit capitulation to that response? In that way, the black man's response has done its work because it addressed the white woman at a discursive level where everything—every single word—was discernible to her. The response produced, it is possible to speculate, the recognition that one does not ask a faculty member at an Ivy League institution to take a second job—or a third, or a . . .—unless one is fully prepared to be confounded (to be found out) because of one's misapprehensions. In Cayuga Heights, it is best to presume—if you are driving a Volvo (or a Subaru)—that everyone, even, or, especially, the laboring black man, is a professor. (Or, just for a moment to generalize the Cayuga Heights encounter, if you're a white man or woman driving around in, say, Austin, Texas, or Palo Alto, California, do not take it as a given that the brown-skinned man mowing the lawn is available for hire. He could very well be a professor or an attorney mowing his own lawn; that might be the best premise from which to begin. The Cayuga Heights encounter is, as will be reflected on later, entirely unexceptional.) Politically, this is precisely what is impossible for the white woman; philosophically, this is absolutely necessary. It is best, for the white woman in this instance, to begin with the presumption that thinking is ubiquitous, because it is impossible to know where we will encounter thinking. Follow the Boy Scout motto when it comes to thinking: "Be Prepared:" You never know when you'll encounter it, you never know when you'll need it. This does not mean, however, that the white woman—figured here metonymically (because the question could as easily have come from the white man)—will not (continue to) harbor the illusion that all black men are laborers, that all black men in Cayuga Heights (and elsewhere, of course; brown or Asian men too) can be summoned, in the most cursory fashion, and offered casual labor. As Baldwin writes, "there is a great deal of power involved in the white man's naïveté"[45]—indifference to the black man comes easily to his white counterpart.

It is, then, not only the elocution (a clear, emphatic speaking) of "faculty" that silenced this woman. It is, rather, that the black man spoke like (one might imagine) a Cornell faculty member is supposed to speak. How was the white woman to know that the black man mistaken for, treated as, a casual laborer, or worse, was more than the sum total of his work clothes? How was she to know that this black man was, sartorially, at any rate, dissembling? What is to be done, linguistically, anyway, when it turns out that the black man in work clothes is a professor? With a PhD in literature, which makes language the very stuff of his everyday professional existence? Who knows where we will find ourselves confronted by thinking? Better to trust ourselves to thinking and, more importantly, even, be willing to interrogate our Unthought, always.

It is the impossibility of knowing where, how, and in what "form" thinking will present itself that made matters worse for the white woman. What a shock to the white woman the act of misrecognition must be, to learn that she is laboring under a misconception in its relation to the black man. What a shock when the white person learns that the black person is, it turns

45. James Baldwin, "Stranger in the Village," in *Collected Essays* (New York: Library Classics of America, 1998), 122.

out, only "masquerading" as a menial laborer, because what he really practices is linguistic facility. The black man becomes, immediately, unrecognizable when he shows command of language and, by far the worst, possesses (an attribute valued by no profession so much as comics) the unfortunate gift of timing. It is not simply what the black man says or how he says it; all that matters is when he says it. Carpe diem: it produces that rare political conjuncture when the black man speaks in grammatically impugning sentences—in a single pithy sentence, moreover, that is full of linguistic discipline and political authority.

In this sentence, the white woman's unreflective, unthinking thrust is met with the black man's fatal linguistic parry. Because of this sentence, the white woman is unable to produce a riposte to him. In the face of his statement, the white woman is reduced to silence—or the self-indictment that is a hasty, unceremonious departure. This silencing of the white woman follows the insertion of difference (and *différance*—an original delay, between answer and departure, in this instance) into the encounter between him and her: in exposing the routine inquiry (the question, which is really an unthinking command, that is not reflected upon; is it possible to think when one commands?) as unthinking (the Unthought), the thinking response reveals the violence that is always potentially present, always potentially threatening, in the "order of the voice."

Or, in the white woman's terms, dis-order has been inserted through the black man's voice. His verbal conciseness and precision have emphatically, but politely, inverted her sense of order—that is, the white woman's authority has been undone, her mode of comprehending the world has been rudely exposed. The violent force located within the exchange between question and answer has been turned against the white woman. This violence that, we can say conclusively, did not come from the black man (it was directed at him) but was turned, economically and surely, by him into a dis-ordered articulation. The dis-ordered articulation destabilizes the white woman's understanding of the established order; the dis-ordered articulation refuses the terms of the rhetorical exchange between white and black. In its economy (every word, every single word, knows its place; there is no superfluity; there is complete grammatical command—"Only if you can match my Cornell faculty salary"—eight words, bearing a lifetime of thinking within them) and its precision (knowing when to say what; knowing, this is crucial, what *not* to say), his dis-ordered speaking issues a political sanction of the highest order. The efficacy of that sanction is unmistakably audible in the white woman's silence. Thinking, in this encounter, is what renders not-thinking speechless.

The difference, in this instance, between the casual inquiry and the thinking response bears the conceptual imprint of what Derrida calls "reserve" ("strategically nicknamed *trace, reserve,* or *différance*").[46] Difference (and *différance*) is thinkable only as a severe kind of reserve—in other contexts, when we wish to denote a high degree of self-control, we might name it "discipline" (not in Foucault's sense, or Bentham's either), especially when anyone—it could be the white man or the black woman—is confronted with extreme provocation, which might take the form of, say, disrespect, contempt, or humiliation.

The effect of "faculty" (thinking), as a metonym (for those eight words, for what was *not* said), is to posit reserve as a "disciplined" holding back that is also, at the very same time, a carefully calibrated rhetorical unleashing. To reserve, then, is not, as is commonly said, to "reserve judgment"—to wait until all the facts have been gathered. It is, rather, to judge harshly in a language that is viscerally understood—the white woman

46. Derrida, *Of Grammatology,* 93.

knows that she has been summarily judged. However, the language of reserve remains, at the level of thinking, of having been thought, unrecognizable to the white woman, because she has been judged according to the terms of dis-order. Those eight words issue from the black man's thinking; moreover, they issue from a terrain inhospitable—even hostile—to the white woman's terms. Having been so indicted, having been found wanting (that is, not thinking), her only possible rejoinder is silence (followed by a philosophically induced deracination), and through that silence, she incriminates itself.

To reserve is to issue judgment in terms that cannot be refuted—there is no possibility of appeal. There is in the mobilization of reserve, then, something of Hegel's notion of "irreducible difference": an uncompromising intolerance for the unthinking speech act. The refusal to accede to the unthinking speech act means that the casual inquiry cannot be, under any circumstances, reconciled to the response produced out of thinking—not-thinking ≠ (is never =) thinking. In the Cayuga Heights encounter, that refusal takes the form of a forceful, gnomic, and enigmatic articulation. It is, however, an entirely apropos articulation. The effect of reserve, then, is that language is never so precise or finely honed as when it is marshaled in the cause of reserve. (As Heidegger so memorably reminds us in "Brief über den Humanismus," "language is the house of Being.")[47] The thinking of the disciplined will silently punish the (question of the) unthinking (which is simultaneously evocative of and entirely distinct from the Unthought);

47. In "Letter on Humanism," Heidegger clearly establishes the relation between thinking and Being: "Thinking accomplishes the relation of Being to the essence of man. It does not make or cause the relation. Thinking brings this relation to Being solely as something handed over to it from Being." Martin Heidegger, "Letter on Humanism," in *Basic Writings*, 217.

to Be in the "house of language" is to ruthlessly command language.

To render this encounter in an incomplete, cautionary, Heideggerian idiom, be careful of what you ask: "Questions are paths toward an answer. If the answer could be given it would consist in a transformation of thinking, not in a propositional about a matter of stake."[48] Be careful of what you ask if you have not thought about what you are asking, have not thought about the effect of what you are about to ask; be careful of the question, unless it is approached as the "path toward an answer." But, be even more careful if you think you (already) know the possible answer(s) to your question (if you are not willing to move beyond the "propositional statement" that is the question); if you have not thought beyond yes or no; if you have not thought beyond acquiescence; if you are not willing to be "transformed" through thinking—"transformed" into thinking, aware of the "injunction" that is inherent in all thinking. This political caution catches something of the withholding tone that St. Paul issues in his First Letter to the Corinthians: "Anyone who claims to know something does not yet have the necessary knowledge" (I Corinthians 8:2). Paul is cautioning his audience about the perils of love and the difficulty of marriage. However, audible, for our purposes, is the way in which Paul establishes the condition of speaking: the ground for the question is "necessary knowledge." The question must proceed from "knowledge"; the question can only begin with—in—thinking; the question is always shadowed—and limned—by the force of Heidegger's Unthought.

Reserve is an articulation that holds itself, with good reason, to an exacting standard. Reserve is demanding because the

---

48. Martin Heidegger, "The End of Philosophy and the Task of Thinking," in *Basic Writings*, 431.

subject recognizes that this holding-back-that-is-not-a-holding-back is the only way in which it can preserve itself through language. It is only through reserve that the Other can maintain self-respect, retain a sense of ipseity ("selfness") that will allow the Other to be in the world with integrity. Without reserve, it would be impossible to think, because the Other is not fully (as none of us ever are) in command of the situation as the Other would like to be. This is a difficulty Marx understands so well in the *Eighteenth Brumaire of Louis Bonaparte*—"Men make their own history, but they do not make it just as they please; they do not make it under circumstances chosen by themselves."[49] We do not make history under conditions of our own choosing. (In this regard, reserve and discipline border precariously on repression—anger, any drive toward violence, must be tamped down, kept in check. We know, however, that such a tamping down is only possible for so long; we know that violence will, in some form or another, make its presence felt. It is the event—that act of political disruption that is impossible to know in advance but is always expected and, because of this, never quite anticipated—that unsettles, in the work of Frantz Fanon, the colonizer, because the colonizer can never be sure when the colonized will act or what will impel the colonized into action;[50] it is the prospect of the event that gives Fanon's work its political force and philosophical urgency in *Le Damnés de la Terre*. The unpredictable predictability of the event is what

49. Karl Marx, "The Eighteenth Brumaire of Louis Bonaparte," in *The Karl Marx Reader,* ed. Robert C. Tucker (New York: W. W. Norton, 1978), 595.

50. On the other hand, in his essay "Concerning Violence," Fanon warns of the expedient ways in which the newly independent black government can mobilize this potentiality: "In this arid phase of national life, the so-called period of austerity, the success of their depredations is swift to call forth the violence and anger of the people." Frantz Fanon, *The Wretched of the Earth* (New York: Grove Press, 1968), 48.

makes the—perpetual—threat of the event the wretched of the earth's greatest political asset.)

No wonder, then, given the burden that the language of reserve must bear, that Heidegger assigns language such a critical role in his essay "Bauen Wohnen Denken": "It is language that tells us about the essence of a thing, provided that we respect language's own essence."[51] The "essence" of reserve can only be discerned by "respecting" the precision of its form—its economy, its efficiency as a political rejoinder, its power to sanction and to neutralize; its discipline. However, what must never be lost sight of is the potentiality of reserve to issue to the white woman, when she is least expecting it, a call to thinking.

51. Heidegger, *Basic Writings,* 348.

"Foreign to Its Own Spontaneity"

> The voice is *heard* (understood)—that is undoubt-
> edly what is called conscience—closest to the self
> as the absolute effacement of the signifier: pure
> auto-affection that necessarily has the form of time
> and which does not borrow from outside itself, in
> the world or in "reality," any necessary signifier,
> any substance of expression foreign to its own
> spontaneity. It is the unique experience of the sig-
> nified producing itself spontaneously, from within
> the self, and nevertheless, as signified concept, in
> the element of ideality or universality.
> —JACQUES DERRIDA, *Of Grammatology*

THROUGH RESERVE, the white woman's question is turned
against itself and returned as nothing less than an indictment
of her; through this indictment, she is, at once and beyond the
shadow of a doubt, made the inheritor—the recipient—of her
own inquiry and held captive by the failure of thinking. There
is nothing for her to do but judge herself in the most resonant
silence. This silence irrupts into a series of questions, one concatenated to the o/Other, without respite: how does the white
woman respond to this silence, a silence she herself produced
but whose effects completely dis-ordered her view of the world,

this silence that bristles with invective? What does she hear in that silence? What is the silence saying, relentlessly, silently, to her? (This means, of course, that the "silence"—the lack of anything to say in response to the response—is never without its own distinctive audibility. The silence speaks.) How does she discern herself in this silence that she has wrought, that she has brought—imposed—on herself? What, and this is the crucial question, does this silence make her confront? If anything? (The lack of a thinking about the silence is the greatest failure of the white woman. In and through her silence, she stands deliberately against thinking.)

The white woman's silencing of herself leads, directly, to the following questions: is to be speechless to be without any language that is grounded in thinking? Is the final effect of not thinking speechlessness? It will not matter that this silence was initiated in "innocence" ("auto-affection"—regard for the self that is resilient but, finally, unsustainable); it will not mater that she will surely assert that "all" she did was make a "harmless" "offer"—where is the harm in that? She had no ill intent, surely everyone must be aware of that. The "harm," as it were, derives from the insularity produced by "auto-affection" because it is a mode of being that does not "borrow from outside itself." This is a self that does not, that does see the need to think itself, a self that seeks no "transformation" into thinking.

The white woman resists "any substance of expression that is foreign to [her] own spontaneity" because she subscribes to her own "unique experience"—her capacity to reproduce herself "spontaneously from within [her]self." Here, for the purposes of this discussion, Derrida's critique can be seen as a broadside aimed at the very heart of the project of bourgeois self-sufficiency. In modernity, the bourgeoisie imagines itself infinitely capable of producing and then reproducing it-self from within itself. "Ideality or universality," which might be rendered here as a fetishized, pristine conception of the world (girded by a strong sense that this is how the world is, and if it isn't, then it is how the world should be), is a powerful bourgeois fiction. In Derrida's terms, the "signified" is the world as the object which the bourgeoisie will perfect—the world is the object in need of bourgeoisie perfecting—but also the "signified" as the object that can "produce itself spontaneously, from within the self." The danger, however, in the "absolute effacement of the signifier" points to the bankruptcy at the core of the bourgeois project: it cannot be sustained because it lacks even the where-withal to properly name itself—the bourgeoisie seeks to "efface" every trace of what is its own undertaking. The bourgeoisie seeks, to coin an awkward phrase (and mixes, to boot, conceptual metaphors, Gramsci and Freud), the hegemony of repression to keep the questions out of sight, out of earshot, and out of, as it were, mind; domination without self-interrogation, rendered in the idiom of Cayuga Heights, domination (that bears perilously on abject—unthought—subjugation) through silence. The bourgeoisie imagines that the hegemony of repression will render the "signifier" superfluous—it will make nothing of the work of clarifying, naming, that the signifier does. This is an illusion; this is fertile ground for the Unthought.

However, the bourgeoisie is intuitively correct in its desire to suppress the signifier. The signifier introduces, bears within itself, the force of language, and because the signifier cannot be controlled, it makes the object—the signified—imminently susceptible to the force of language. Contained within the signifier is "spontaneity," the force of language, announcing the arrival of discourse, both of which are antagonistic, and even openly hostile, to the object as object—as signified. The signifier is constitutively averse to prescription or proscription; that is why we have long considered it "free floating," which it both, of course, is and is not—the signifier is never entirely uncoupled, liberated, from the signified. The signifier returns, in this case, in the form of the black man's linguistic precision. The hegemony of repression is vulnerable to nothing so much as what it wants to keep locked away: the Other as the bearer of thinking that stands in contradistinction to its own not-thinking. The white woman's Unthought emerges, in part, through the black man's thinking; her Unthought emerges in no small measure through her own question; she is responsible for the unveiling of her Unthought.

The effect of "spontaneity" is the unpredictability of its response. Like any political event, the spontaneous is true only to itself; like the political, the spontaneous cannot know how or to what it will respond; or, more explicable but only accessible through what Alain Badiou names "supplementarity,"[52] is why the political event occurs when it does. This means that nothing, including, least of all, thinking, is foreign to spontaneity. If this is the case, then we must never be surprised—even as we are apprehended in and by our thinking—at what "spontaneity" yields. If nothing is "foreign to spontaneity," then we must expect thinking—even when we imagine ourselves not to be thinking—to manifest (make itself audible, reveal itself, speak as itself)—not only to surprise us; we must be—before ourselves, before we are surprised—open to the "foreign." The "foreign," in this way, challenges any notion of what is "native" to thought. The force of "spontaneity" derives from its ability to refuse categorization. Thinking cannot be divided into "native" and "foreign," indigenous or imported, proper or improper (sign and signified), Self and Other, white and black; thinking

---

52. See Alain Badiou, *Ethics: An Essay on the Understanding of Evil*, trans. Peter Hallward (New York: Verso, 2002).

is indefatigably, resolutely, mischievously, indivisible—it leaves out nothing.

The "spontaneous," which is of course never the consequence of happenstance but the effect of thinking, retains to itself the right to gather everything, every thinking, into itself. Because the "spontaneous" is true to thinking and nothing else, it understands Heidegger—as effected through, made possible by, *Was heißt Denken?*—as entirely appropriate in the moment of response. That is to say, there is nothing "foreign" about my turn to Heidegger; Heidegger, we might say, made himself "spontaneously" available to the diasporized heir of the "Senegalese Negro." The black man is open to *Was heißt Denken?* even as he is troubled by, made to think about, Heidegger's political offenses and transgressions, his culpabilities, the injunctions he provokes; and, yes, his polemics too. In the face of all of this, aware of the paradoxes and the joke that is on him, the black man remains resolutely—absolutely—open to Martin Heidegger.

Thinking avails itself, through the commitment to thinking thinking, in the moment of record. Where a discourse grounded in a narrow critique of racism might view Heidegger as inappropriate, offensive, even, or, much worse, extraneous to the thinking of race and racism, the effect of thinking is to show the efficacy, and the utter usefulness, of thinking qua thinking. (This does not mean, as has just been mentioned and of which we will see more shortly, that a certain instructive irony does not obtain from the very beginning in Heidegger's "emergence" as the figure in and through which thinking articulates itself.) Understood as such, the defining characteristic of thinking is that it will not admit to the possibility that any "substance of expression," emerging from within the self or not, lies beyond the purview of thinking; as such, thinking stands against what

Derrida names the "desire for rigorous non-contamination."[53] The axiomatics of thinking is that Heidegger, or any other thinker, is always to hand, whether or not we want a Heidegger to be in such close attendance. However, for Heidegger or any other thinker to be to hand, we need only (which is to say, "only" must be understood as everything) to have thought thinking for thinking to make itself "spontaneously," which is to say strategically (when it really matters), available. There is nothing accidental to how (Heidegger), when (carpe diem), and in what grammatical order (precision, discipline of language) thinking articulates itself.

And thinking because of Heidegger lends thinking, in the Cayuga Heights instance, the Nietzschean quality of "untimeliness"—reaching for *Was heißt Denken?* makes of my thinking an "untimely meditation," a meditation that goes hard against the grain of what is expected.[54] Of what, specifically, is expected racially from both the white woman's and the black discursive paradigm; the former anticipates acquiescence, subservience, and a lack of rhetorical facility; the latter is unprepared for anything other than the invocation of a canonical figure— the expectation of a racially grounded intellectual epistemology and solidarity, shall we call it? My "instinctive," "unthinking" turn to Heidegger suggests that there might be something untimely about thinking. There is philosophical value in the

53. Derrida, *Of Spirit,* 10.
54. I have in mind here the meditation on Schopenhauer ("Schopenhauer as educator") in which Nietzsche shows how valuable Schopenhauer's work was for him—for his imagination, for his understanding of self, for the dissonance between Schopenhauer's life and his philosophy, and so on—despite his disagreements with Schopenhauer. Friedrich Nietzsche, *Untimely Meditations* (New York: Cambridge University Press, 1997).

untimely because it is the thinker who is out of vogue, pilloried, dismissed (consider Derrida's critique of Sartre—"He made so many mistakes"; "I admire his sense of justice but I don't owe him anything in philosophy"—damned with the faint phrase that is his commitment to justice; such is Sartre's fate at Derrida's hands), who might, precisely because he is unfashionable, make us think in ways we could not have foreseen. It is the untimely thinker who, because there is nothing propitious about him presenting himself to us, makes us think as we would otherwise not have been able to think. In this case, Heidegger's untimeliness is of the singular variety: he is the untimely thinker who brings my thinking into being. The force of the Heideggerian untimely is, ironically, that it produces a timely thinking; a thinking entirely addressed to the political demands of the moment. The untimely is the gift of an ironic history because the untimely can, despite every expectation, be said to know nothing so much as its own time.

The Only Thing Essential to Thinking Is Thinking

THIS STATEMENT IS SO IMPORTANT that it must be phrased declaratively, even stridently: the only thing that is essential to thinking is thinking. The defining characteristic of thinking is that it excludes nothing and, in so doing, exposes itself to everything. In this way, thinking is (Unthought and) "un-disciplined": it runs the risk of including within itself everything, a risk constitutive of thinking, and in taking this risk, it exposes itself to everything. In so doing, thinking insulates itself against nothing. "Therefore," says Heidegger, "we always must seek out thinking, and its burden of thought, in the element of its multiple meanings, else everything will remain closed to us."[55] Heidegger's "burden of thought" begins from the premise that thinking dedicates itself to searching for the "element of its multiple meanings," that it will not admit of the possibility that anything "remain closed" to thinking. There can be, there must be, no prophylaxis against thinking.

Of course, this is not to suggest that thinking is without discrimination. Rather, as we will see shortly, thinking never hesitates when it is necessary to adjudicate, to make judgments, or to order itself. But that, however, is what happens "after" or

55. Heidegger, *Was heißt Denken?*, 71.

in the ever-ongoing work of thinking everything. There is no end to thinking—there is no historical situation we can imagine as "post-thinking." However, the work of judgment, which comes in the presence/present of thinking, can be undertaken only "after" thinking as much as possible. As we well know from the turn of *Was heißt Denken?* to Nietzsche, Plato, and Heraclitus,[56] among others, thinking as much as possible is no small task. And because it is necessary to always to be thinking in order to lay claim to thinking, "after" thinking is best understood as belonging to the aporia; it simply marks an "interruption," a slowing down, a meditation (both timely and untimely) on thinking, if you will, before thinking is taken up fully again. Thinking apprehends itself; it is only possible to think in anticipation of the apprehending that lies on the immediate horizon.

And so, I apprehend my own thinking ("What is most provocative in our thought provoking age is that we are still not thinking") because what did not come to me in the encounter is what apprehends me now. I did not, until now (or, maybe, sometime after, that is, before now but after the encounter), reference or turn to any one of a number of figures who might have been presumed more epistemologically obvious or "appropriate" resources for my response. I did not turn to Malcolm X's famous hypothetical that is, it would seem, more or less tailor-made—rhetorically—for my encounter with the white woman. After all, the question Malcolm X is supposed to have asked offers itself as a paradigmatic resource for my encounter; it stands as the

56. That Heidegger's thinking turns so frequently, and so exclusively, to what we might name Greco-German thinkers, and that the Heidegger "library" excludes the likes of Spinoza and Husserl, both Jewish thinkers, is, Mladen Dolar argued in conversation (pers. comm., Ljubljana, March 2015), one of the major problems with Heidegger's work on thinking—to say nothing, of course, of the particular status Heidegger affords the languages of Greek and German.

perfect retort that went unutilized. The question attributed to Malcolm X is, we remember, "What do you call a nigger with a PhD?" His answer, of course, is famous both for its succinctness (the answer, predictable and yet not)—a single word already iterated, provocatively, in the question—and for its democratic structuring of American racism; the perverse democratizing of the black experience in the United States. His answer, rendered formally, which is to say with a capital *N,* is "Nigger." Malcolm X's answer, which is anti-academic and possibly anti-intellectual too (strange, given that this is a man who came to his epiphanies precisely through and because of one of the monotheistic books), is intended to disabuse educated African Americans (and probably all black people) of the illusion that formal education can insulate them against racism of both the routine (everyday slights and indignities) and structural (as manifested in state institutions) varieties. (Baldwin offers an equivalent sentiment, which resonates with the disposability of black bodies, in "The Evidence of Things Not Seen": "for the State, a nigger is a nigger is nigger, sometimes Mr. or Mrs. or Dr. Nigger." The occasional formality—"Mr. or Mrs. or Dr."—notwithstanding, what remains most legible—audible—is the "State's" definition of black personhood, or nonpersonhood: "a nigger is a nigger is a nigger."[57]) The structure of racism for blacks in the United States cannot be effectively countered by acquiring a PhD. In Malcolm X's terms, American racism cannot be challenged by acquiring "devilish" knowledge. When a black Harvard professor is handled roughly by the Cambridge, Massachusetts, police for "breaking in" to his own home, and then the story becomes the stuff of presidential legend (complete with the erstwhile antagonists making peace over Budweiser

57. Baldwin, "The Evidence of Things Not Seen," in *Collected Essays,* 18.

beer at the White House, hosted by an African American president, himself a graduate of Harvard's law school), it becomes impossible to argue the resonance—and the historic resilience—of Malcolm X's question.

Malcolm X's logic is, in the face of the black professor's vulnerability to the white lawman, irrefutable. All black subjects are equally vulnerable in the face of racism. In different ways, the Cambridge incident (which garnered international attention; I watched it unfold on television in Sydney, Australia, in 2009) and my encounter in Cayuga Heights attest to that. Neither the black man's PhD nor his professorial appointment could, in the encounter, shield him from the white police officer or two white residents of Cayuga Heights. Indeed, what do they call a nigger with a PhD? "Boy" is what I heard echoing softly. "Boy" concatenated to "nigger," echoing a little less softly. Apartheid South Africa and upstate New York, yoked into a relation of, as, racist poetics in *Gespräch*. "Boy" and "nigger," "Nigger" or "*Neger*!": silent, resonant, reverberating, loud, too loud to bear. What the silence makes audible is uncanny.

What did the white couple "hear" in my voice? Did they detect my "foreign" accent in those eight clipped words? Or is it that my South African accent (how many words does it take to mark an accent?) was secondary to a more pressing question: what, or who, to phrase the matter properly, was the source of the precision of the black man's "spontaneity"? Is that what was truly "foreign" to this couple? Was this black man the "signified"—the object of inquiry who would not submit to the terms of the inquiry—that every white woman or man dreads? Did they recognize thinking as that which was articulated in and through my response? How could they know that Martin Heidegger was no more "foreign" to me than the nationalist politics of Malcolm X, the Nation of Islam, or Booker T. Washington?

How could they know that Heidegger was no more "foreign" to me than the short stories of William Trevor or the novels of Toni Morrison?

For my part, how could I not have heard the first line of Morrison's most acclaimed work, *Beloved*: "124 was spiteful"?[58] Now, some days, with a new force since Guy Fawkes Day 2013, our house, "540 Cayuga Heights Road," strikes me as not so much "spiteful" as haunted, as "124 Bluestone Road" was certainly haunted by that unspeakable violence—hauntings that Sethe, Baby Suggs, and Paul D know so well. Hauntings of a different order, I hasten to add; and yet, the thing of it is, every haunting recalls every other haunting. I did not know, when Jane, Ezra, and I moved to Cayuga Heights, that we'd be living so close to Morrison's house on Bluestone Road.

Following Morrison's lead, and the newly unearthed presence of Beloved in my haunted neighborhood, it seems proper to historicize Cayuga Heights as the originating scene. This requires a statement that is a negation: 540 Cayuga Heights Road was not the "original" scene of misapprehension. Neither was my raking the source of the white woman's misapprehension. My identification as Other is not attributable to my raking. To borrow that memorable indictment of Vichy France for disenfranchising the Jews of Algeria (Marshall Pétain's government of Occupation overturned the Crémieux of 1840, which enfranchised French Jews), as issued in Derrida's *Le monolinguisme de l'autre: ou la prosthèse d'origine,* "the withdrawal of French citizenship from the Jews of Algeria, with everything that followed, was the deed of the French alone. They decided that all by themselves, in their heads; they must have been dreaming about it all along; they implemented it all by

58. Toni Morrison, *Beloved* (New York: Plume Fiction, 1988), 3.

themselves."[59] "They," for which the white woman (and the man, the metonymic white couple) stands in, stands as, must have had a figure of the black man in their heads—in their bourgeois illusions—long before they addressed that question to me.

That question was a lifetime in the making. The black man was approached as Other because the black man was, in their heads, all along, as a black man, Other. The Other was Other long before she (they) approached me raking my leaves on my property. I was only approached because I was Other. Any one of my white colleagues who live within shouting distance of 540 Cayuga Heights Road could have been dressed in exactly the same attire and they would not—under any circumstance—have been subjected to this inquiry. In the white couple's logic, the Other can be approached as Other because the Other's mode of being in the world is distinct from that of the white woman or man. Whatever protestations (or apologies, rationalizations, or just a knowing incomprehension) my white colleagues might offer, they know, regardless of how they dress, that my mode of being is distinct from all of theirs. The Other, we can assert, is always susceptible—vulnerable—to the possibility of the "spiteful" encounter. Nothing can insulate the Other from the white Volvo and the hauntings that are loosed when it stops and approaches the black man.

It is necessary, now, I recognize, to insist on this couple's shared culpability. The male passenger said nothing, even though he was closest to me. That is, the white man did not speak against the white woman's question. He acted as if her question were entirely ordinary, so he did what he has, I presume, always done. He went along with it. They came to the

59. Jacques Derrida, *Monolingualism of the Other: Or the Prosthesis of Origin,* trans. Patrick Mensah (Stanford, Calif.: Stanford University Press, 1998), 16.

inquiry together, side by side, literally. Nor did the white man acknowledge my response. Or, if he did, I did not, in turning my back on them sharply, hear him rebuke or disagree with her.

My exchange, then, was never only with the white woman. It was, rather, a triangulated encounter, in which one silence (the woman's in response to my question) was compounded by another (the white man's). Theirs was the silence of complicity, silences joining together in the face of the Other's rejoinder. How many silences were dis-ordered? One? Two? None?

The correct answer, however unknowable it might be, must begin in the knowledge that there was at least one silence. (The answer, then, is, at least one. But more likely, it is one plus; that is always the formula.) The unarguable silence, however, is mine. That is because the question of silence does not end with the colluding white couple but extends to (begins with?) me. I was silent in relation to the canonical black figures—here *black* must be understood as referencing African American, African, and diasporic African figures. I did not draw upon them as a resource, not in the first instance, as I have already stated.

I did not draw upon Malcolm X. And that is no small matter. I remember pondering that, but only afterward. I only turned to Malcolm X in thinking about why I did not turn to him. When I turned my back on the couple, I went back to raking. However, I was no longer simply gathering the leaves into a pile. I was by no means fully tuned in to the edification of my soul, but neither was I agitated. I was already overtaken by thinking, or, as is equally likely, extending myself into Heidegger's conundrum on thinking in *Was heißt Denken?* Or, I was accepting—had accepted—Heidegger's "gift" of thinking: "Thinking is thinking only when it pursues whatever speaks *for* a subject."[60] I accepted Heidegger's gift because he provoked me to think

60. Heidegger, *Was heißt Denken?,* 13; original emphasis.

about what had spoken "for" me as a "subject." I had "pursued" Heidegger, called to him, not to any other. A felicitous act, an act which provoked me to ask why my thinking had led me where it did.

Heidegger, not Malcolm X, had spoken for me. Heidegger, not Frantz Fanon, whose critiques of colonialism find resonance in my work in other moments. My response did not recall that famous scene in *Peau noire, masques blancs* when, in Lyon (where he studied) or Paris, the young Martinican student Fanon is apprehended by a little white girl with the phrase that bristles with an uncomprehending recognition: "Look, a Negro!" "Mama, see the Negro! I'm frightened."[61] (Despite visiting the village of Leukerbad, Switzerland, a few times, Baldwin recalls being hailed in a way similar to Fanon: "I remain as much a stranger today as I was the first day I arrived, and the children shout *Neger! Neger!* as I walk along the streets."[62]) In Cayuga Heights, it might have been rendered by the driver and the passenger in that Volvo as, "Look, a black man who will work for us!" In no way was the white couple "frightened" of me, but I remained as much a "Negro" as Fanon was on that street in mid-twentieth-century Paris or Lyon, or as Baldwin was in Leukerbad. The Martinican in colonial France is a source of anxiety, capable of "frightening" the young white girl; the "Negro" in Ithaca is immediately raced, which then allows him to be assigned to the class of menial labor. The black man in Ithaca cannot disturb the racial equilibrium in Ithaca at least not until he responds to the white woman's question.

To be black is to live, as a matter of course, with the possibility—it is closer, in truth, to an inevitability—of misrecognition.

61. Frantz Fanon, *Black Skin, White Mask,* trans. Charles Lam Markmann (New York: Grove Press, 1967), 112.
62. Baldwin, "Stranger in the Village," 118.

It is to live with the prospect of being named, of being subsumed into a racial–racist (Negro!–*Neger!*) or racist–economic (menial laborer, lumpenproletariat, *gastarbeiter*) category. But, again, Fanon's and my interpellations are of a different order, but they animate each other; these addresses are from one black man to another/an-Other, addresses that make nothing of their contextual (Paris/Lyon and Ithaca; the European metropolis and the small American college town) and temporal differences (encounters separated by more than fifty years). I've read, taught, and written on Fanon, but I did not turn to him, even though I could, in retrospect, hear him echoing across the decades: "I was battered down by tom-toms, cannibalism, intellectual deficiency, fetishism, racial defects, slave-ships."[63] We share, he and I, in the view of the white girl or the elderly woman, the presumption of "intellectual deficiency" and "racial defects."

Heidegger, not W. E. B. Du Bois, whose oft-quoted opening line of "Of the Dawn of Freedom," the second chapter of *The Souls of Black Folk*—"The problem of the twentieth-century is the problem of the color line"[64]—retains, more than a century later, its declarative force. As a critique of American racism, it is difficult to imagine a more bracing line. I did not draw on Du Bois, a figure whose work is central to founding the project of Cornell University's Africana Studies, where I hold an appointment. In any case, I was being viewed less as a "problem" and more as someone caught on the "wrong side" of the "color line." In Ithaca, it's a rather remarkable line in that it divides those who reimburse for labor from those who "seek" it, even those, like me, who do not even know that they're seeking "another job."

63. Fanon, *Black Skin*, 112.
64. Du Bois, *Souls of Black Folk*, 16.

Martin Heidegger, not Toni Morrison, was spinning around and around in my head—Morrison, a Cornell University graduate (MA, 1955), the writer who plumbs the bitter, life-sustaining depths of black life; Morrison, whose characters lend a narrative force to the history of black life in the United States.

Heidegger, and Heidegger alone, splendid in his solitude, occupied me—speaking for me, allowing me to speak in such a way that was faithful to thinking. We do not know how thinking will order—will organize—itself. Thinking is true only to itself; it draws whence it chooses. Thinking is sovereign; it decides for the (unexceptional) exception, to misquote Carl Schmitt.

On second thought, maybe I was entirely out of sorts and utterly unable to shake the effects of the encounter just passed. The encounter that was passing through me was an encounter of such an order that it made me think about thinking as I had never thought about thinking before. Heidegger: "We come to know what it means to think when we ourselves are thinking. If our attempt is to be successful, we must be ready to learn thinking."[65]

Maybe, in that moment after the encounter that could not be disarticulated from the encounter itself, I needed to turn to thinking, to "learn thinking," more urgently than I ever had before in my life. "We do not know," Heidegger says in *Was heißt Denken?*, "what thinking is. But we do know when we are not thinking." Without Martin Heidegger, I am convinced, as is surely patently clear by now, that it would not have been possible for me to have produced the response that disabled the white woman—the white couple. Martin Heidegger saved my life.

My response was entirely the product of thinking. My answering Heidegger's call manifests itself most visibly in my refusal

65. Heidegger, *Basic Writings*, 369.

to accede—to submit—to an entirely different rhetorical reper-
toire: Malcolm X's, Fanon's, Morrison's, Du Bois's. (Du Bois, as
we shall see in a moment, did offer, after the encounter, a kind
of solidarity—maybe even a kind of solace.) This, quite rightly,
provokes the question, Why?

Every question is in itself an epistemological problem,
because no one knows where the question, any question, might
lead ("transformation" into thinking is difficult to achieve).
We do not know what the question that begins with the white
woman will open up. Even in the silence, however, we can
assert, with Derrida, that the "voice is *heard* (understood)."[66]
In the dis-order of the voice, we are free to assert, the voice is
"understood" with an unrelenting clarity. In silence, the voice
is "heard," because every timber echoes, loudly, in the silence.
We hear so much better because of the silence. It is possible,
in this silence, to hear Heidegger's voice as a call to intellectual ir-responsibility: to turn away from canonical black thinkers, figures whose primary commitment is to the consideration
of race.

Heidegger's is a call that resonates profoundly (and with
a deeply personal, and psychological, aspect) in this context,
where the fidelity to one thinker over others presents itself as
such a wrenching—and yet not—difficulty: "One thing is necessary, though, for a face-to-face converse with the thinkers:
clarity about the manner in which we encounter them. Basi-
cally, there are only two possibilities: either go to their encounter, or to go counter to them."[67] Here there is no escaping it,
because Heidegger demands an explanation. In the "face-to-
face encounter with the thinkers," it is absolutely necessary to
account for why one goes one way and not another. (Audible,

---

66. Derrida, *Of Grammatology*, 20.
67. Heidegger, *Was heißt Denken?*, 77.

interrupting, here is Foucault's question about the economy of thought: "What is the cost?" What is the cost of thinking Heidegger and not anyone else?) Heidegger demands, as he brings us "face-to-face with the thinkers," that every one of us declare ourselves. Heidegger's is a call for specificity, for clarity, for ruthless calculation. He asks of me, Why is it that Martin Heidegger made the response possible and no one else? Heidegger demands that thinking begin with thinking—that is where his felicity lies. Not so with Du Bois and Fanon, not so with Malcolm X and Morrison: their first loyalty, understandably, is to race. They are committed to thinking race. Race may be my subject, but I come to race through thinking. For Fanon and Morrison, race is "A." For me, it is "B." In the moment of the encounter, I went with Heidegger—let's afford me some volition, just for a second—for whom thinking is, and always will be, "A." "A" trumps "B," but this does not require, for me, that I abandon "B." My "B" is close to my "A," but it is only close. An ordering such as mine demands an accounting because, as Derrida says in his reflections on Heidegger, "after the disasters have happened," there are "unprecedented responsibilities [for] 'thought' and action."[68] The only way to be "responsible" to thought is to remind oneself, repeatedly, of the Heideggerian "disasters."

To (be made to) think in this "disastrous" way is to begin—(to know, expressly) what is at stake about race, philosophy, thinking itself—with the question, Why Martin Heidegger? This question, there can be no denying, is the source of a great deal of perturbation. It reveals the turbulence that is unleashed by my turn to Heidegger. The first line of interrogation is an obvious but by no means unjustified one: why does the black man's response, his precise turn of phrase, come

68. Derrida, *Of Spirit,* 40.

from Heidegger? Heidegger—now more than ever a scandalous figure—how can it be that Martin Heidegger was the source of my "salvation"?

Well, because we've arrived at a strange occurrence in the history of philosophy. We've arrived at that moment when the joke is on Heidegger. According to the Lacanians, the remarkable thing about the Heidegger corpus, a voluminous body of work to be sure, is that it does not contain a single joke. Although the Cayuga Heights encounter does not rise to the level that the Lacanians demand, there is still something paradoxical, and a little funny, I tell myself, about my turn to him. The joke is on the Nazi philosopher, because it is his insistence on thinking that enables the black man to rebut the white woman. Heidegger, the anti-Semite who invokes the "Senegalese negro" as a pedagogical prop, puts me, the black man from southern Africa, in a position to counter a racist question. What could be more paradoxical than that? This is what Heidegger's fidelity to the "Unthought" has wrought: the black man silencing the question conceived in a racist consciousness. How could I not, simultaneously, thank Heidegger and allow myself a historical chuckle?[69] And confronting my Unthought allows me to

69. And to think, furthermore, if I might be permitted an intensification of the paradox in English, Heidegger, as is well known, considered Greek and German the only languages properly fitted for thought. Here it is also worth noting Derrida's argument with Heidegger's argument (as a part of which we should recall again Derrida's commitment to translation), most memorably offered in the *Der Spiegel* interview. It is only possible to think in one's own language, Heidegger maintained; Derrida, of course (here *Monolingualism* is the exemplary text), insisted that we can only think in the language of the Other. The Cayuga Heights encounter lends an element, to phrase the matter in the overdetermined terms of anti-/colonialism, because here it is the Other who mobilizes—animates—the language of the Self (Heidegger, and Derrida too) against the Self (the white woman).

add a wry, sardonic edge to the Lacanian critique of him too. It is possible to extend the joke to that other thinker so beloved by Lacanians, Hegel, because one could say that the joke has the structure of a Hegelian triad. First, there is the thesis, "There is not a single joke in Heidegger"; followed by the antithesis, "What kind of a life is it that was saved by a man with no humor whatsoever?"; culminating in the *Aufhebung* synthesis: "The joke is on Heidegger!"[70] And on me, of course.[71]

70. I am indebted to these notions of the joke to Lidija Šumah. She pointed these out after I presented an earlier version of this argument at the University of Ljubljana in March 2015.

71. Derrida is—how shall I put it?—at least a little preoccupied with the idea of Heidegger and humor. Derrida is kind to Heidegger in this regard, but his "affection" is tempered by considerable caution, aimed, it would seem, at Derrida himself. To wit: "According to one's mood, [Heidegger] calls for either the most serious or the most amused reflections. (That's what I like about Heidegger. When I think about him, when I read him, I'm aware of both these vibrations at the same time. It's always horribly dangerous and wildly funny, certainly grave and a bit comical.)" Derrida, *Of Spirit,* 68.

Who Thinks?

THE LACANIAN JOKE is only the "culmination" of the first level of critique. The second, and this leads to a series of concatenated questions, is negatively phrased but full of invective and replete with indictment. Why not, in the moment of the encounter, invoke Du Bois or Morrison? Does the turning to Heidegger stand as an implicit accusation? That Malcolm X and Fanon do not think? If thinking orders itself, orders itself through our thinking, then the turn to Heidegger cannot stand as anything but a Heideggerian declarative: I went, in the moment of record (in what I have named the "encounter"), with the "encounter." I went "counter to them"—Malcolm X, Du Bois, Morrison, Fanon. And that was, there is no getting around it, a profoundly philosophical choice—and, as always, philosophy has implications for politics. No one exemplifies this better, as I have just delineated, than Heidegger

However, to answer the question, Why Heidegger? it is necessary to understand the precise terms of the choice. To proclaim my choice an indictment or even a judgment of any other thinker would be to undermine the philosophical specificity of my preference for the "encounter." Though there might, of course, be nothing simple about this issue, it is still possible to offer a simple statement: it is a matter of philosophical recognition, and there can be no gainsaying the importance of that.

I turned to Martin Heidegger, or Martin Heidegger came to me, or Martin Heidegger made his thinking available to me, for one reason above all others. Of all the philosophers I have turned to, of all the thinkers I am familiar with, of all theorists I read, Martin Heidegger is the only one who, explicitly, sets himself the task of thinking about thinking. (Foucault, in the "Man and His Doubles" chapter of *Les Mots et Les Choses,* comes close, but in his meditations on thinking, Foucault sounds awfully Heideggerian. And, as I indicated earlier, there is always the persistent shadow that is Descartes.) Heidegger could not, as we have seen, be clearer about this in *Was heißt Denken?* It is the task of thinking thinking that he sets us—who else asks us to think thinking? It is up to us, in this regard, to "match" Heidegger in his dedication to thinking. We can only match Heidegger if we can match his efforts to think about why thinking is all we should think about.

At the core of the encounter in Cayuga Heights is the recognition that a critical part of thinking is to listen to—to hear—ourselves thinking. Hearing has two consequences: first, by paying careful attention to what the white woman says, both before and during her speaking, we can think our way to the proper response; and second, if we listen, we can hear the terms of the thoughts that "come to us." To hear thinking in this way is grasp how this thinking always comes to us from another place, maybe several other places; it comes to us from another thinker, from our thinking that thinker. It comes to us when we least expect it, so we should always expect thinking to propel us into thinking about thinking. To borrow a line from Derrida's critique of *Geist,* thinking is "heterogeneous from the origin."[72] Thinking knows itself as, must know itself as, "contaminated" ("heterogeneous") from the very beginning;

72. Ibid., 108.

that is, thinking draws from well beyond itself, that is, from well beyond what would, at first glance, appear a "good fit" or a "natural turn." Thinking resists any delimitation; thinking follows where thinking leads. To offer *Aufhebung* in a slightly different light: to think the Cayuga Heights encounter, it is necessary to both *vermeiden* (avoid) Fanon and Du Bois and to preserve them, to apprehend their status as "nonthinkers"[73] so that it might be possible to think, and then think race, because it is precisely their *Rassengedanke* that troubles me into a thinking in which race "contaminates" all (my) thinking. Or Malcolm X and Morrison "remind" me that my thinking is, from the very first, before itself, already contaminated.

In the concluding paragraph to "Of the Training of Black Men," Du Bois's essay on black life behind the Veil, the African American sociologist captures the affirmative nature of the black subject's predicament. It is entirely possible to argue for "On the Training of Black Men" as Du Bois's meditation on thinking. However, what is unmistakable in this context is Du Bois's insistence on his right, as a black subject, to claim fully his Enlightenment inheritance: "I sit with Shakespeare and he winces not. Across the color line I move arm in arm with Balzac and Dumas."[74] In this regard, Du Bois has it easy. No sustainable argument (let us, for now, recognize that it also contains an "ethical" component) can be offered that seeks to

73. To name figures such as DuBois and Fanon "non-thinkers" in this regard is to designate them critical philosophers of race who do not make the thinking of thinking their project; this designation constitutes both a recognition of their Derridean proclivities—thinking what Heidegger does not—and a critique of "giving up" thinking as such; all of which, of course, returns us to the philosophical singularity—the philosophical force—of *Was heißt Denken?*

74. W. E. B. Du Bois, "Of the Training of Black Men," in *Souls of Black Folk*, 82.

deny Du Bois the company of Shakespeare, Dumas, or "Aristotle and Aurelius."[75]

However, when the black man traces his path to thinking through Heidegger, another kind of account is demanded. Du Bois is proclaiming himself a full citizen of modernity, presenting us with an understanding of the Enlightenment as constitutive of the black experience (in all the violence and cultural prospect that constitute that experience) that is shared by other black figures—from Toussaint L'Ouverture to Frederick Douglass, from C. L. R. James to Amy Garvey and Amílcar Cabral; all these figures, but especially Toussaint, and Douglass in the (late) eighteenth and nineteenth centuries, contributed to the Enlightenment project almost as much as their thinking was shaped by it. Heidegger presents, for all the reasons already suggested, a different kind of difficulty, but he also offers his thinking as, in, its singularity. And, always, as a question (that wends, in one way or another, through thinking): what is the cost of thinking through a "contaminated" figure? What does the "contaminated" figure do for one's thinking? What happens, to take up Derrida's question about Heidegger and Trakl, in that "collocution of *Denker*" and *Denker*?[76] What happens in the "collocution" between the black man and the *über* German *Denker*, the *Denker* who locates thinking only in German and Greek? In the process of thinking because of, and with, Heidegger, to borrow from Deleuze and Guattari's proposition in *Qu'est-ce que a philosophie?* (thereby raising a startling possibility), has Heidegger become a "friend"—my "friend"—"in thought"?[77] Is thinking the precondition for friendship? What kind of "untimely" friendship does thinking make possible?

75. Ibid.
76. Derrida, *Of Spirit,* 83.
77. Deleuze and Guattari, *What Is Philosophy?,* 4.

Already thinking—which is also, as has been noted, a form of thanking—Heidegger has made it necessary to address Du Bois in such a way, recalling, to begin with, "On the Training of Black Men," that was not at all discernible in the moment of the Cayuga Heights encounter. At the very least, Heidegger prepares us for the unpredictable nature of thinking. We can never be sure of the form in which thinking will make itself available to us—what the shape and extent of its "contamination" will be. In my case, all of the sources upon which I draw to think the response produced in the Cayuga Heights encounter share the following characteristic: apartheid South Africa, racism in the United States, and Martin Heidegger (thinker, in equal measure, of race as "metaphysical" and "biologistic") are all, each in its own way, "contaminated" resources. Together, these sources made it possible for a disenfranchised, diasporized black man (who has lived almost an equal amount of time in South Africa and the United States) to produce out of his thinking, "provoked"—challenged, enjoined, confronted—by Heidegger, an otherwise unthinkable response.

The three sources are not, of course, all "contaminated" in the same way—they are not politically or epistemologically equivalent to each other; but these contexts do evoke each other, and Heidegger grounds them in, and with, a philosophical urgency. They cannot be made the same, but it is precisely because they are all, in some measure or other, "contaminated" that they become engines for thinking. They derive their urgency from their "contamination." We do not, in the terms of Marx's "Eighteenth Brumaire," come to thinking under conditions of our own choosing. We do not know how we will come to thinking. Nor can we determine, before the encounter itself, in it, or long afterward, which philosopher will bring us to thinking—or if we will come to thinking through thinking as such or through the Unthought; both are equally possible. Neither can one account for how the various forms—thinkers, contexts, their relation to each other—of "contamination" will "interact," how they will inform, shape, inflame, distort, or enable each other; and this is to say nothing of the force of the Unthought. These are all matters for thinking. Most important, however, is the recognition that "contamination," like the untimely, is a force for thinking, not an impediment to it.

The Order of the Voice

> And thus we say "writing" for all that gives rise to
> an inscription in general, whether it is literal or not
> and even if what it distributes in space is alien to
> the order of the voice.
>
> —JACQUES DERRIDA, *Of Grammatology*

The first thought produces the articulation that counts. It is where thought is first found; it tells us if thinking has taken place, if there has been thinking. If there has been, as it were, preparation for just such an encounter, even though there can be no preparation for such an encounter. And yet the Other lives forever in anticipation of such an encounter, which means that the Other has to hand an axiomatic for dealing with the white woman or man. I would have been well within my rights to indict, to unleash a string of expletives, to name the offense in a belligerent way, to make the transgression fully public. I did not. I turned to Heidegger, accepting, as it were, the thought that came from him: "That we retain a concern for care in speaking is all to the good, but it is of no help to us as long as language still serves us even then only as a means of expression. Among all the appeals that we human beings, on our part, can help to be voiced, language is the highest and everywhere the first."[78] Something is at work here: a "concern for speaking" born of the recognition that language, as such, could not "serve only as a means of expression." Something else is at work here: the "order of the voice" that makes of language the "highest and everywhere the first." The voice, as understood through Derrida, commands language—the voice makes language fit for the politics of everyday life; the voice makes language fit the event; the voice is the instrument of language; language finds itself, language comes fully into itself, only in the voice. Language and the voice are ordered by thinking.

To think is to say what is at once not expected and entirely appropriate. It is, to phrase the matter negatively but no less clearly or emphatically, not to say what is expected. I could have said, "You are a racist." Or, "You racist." Or I could have added an expletive, as in, "You f—ing racist." Or, simply, "F— you" or "F— off." I would certainly have been within my rights. I would have been beyond reproach. And yet, that was not what I said. Because Heidegger gives us to understand that to think is to command a language that is not yours but comes not so much to you as from your thinking—it is yours, you have no claim to it, it is at your disposal. Thoughts come to us through thinking: through the language that knows that it is opposed to—is against—not-thinking. This is the language that comes from living with Heidegger. It is because of thinking that one response, one thought, emerges rather than any other.

The voice is ordered by thinking. Does it then follow that thinking finds itself in the voice? If so, is the relationship between thinking and the order of the voice one not only of articulation but of articulation as a mode of necessary repression? What is it about thinking that, in my response, inhibits,

78. Martin Heidegger, "Building Dwelling Thinking," in *Poetry, Language, Thought,* 146.

prohibits, disciplines, enjoins, censors—which is itself a form of intellectual and archival withholding ("reserve")—Malcolm X, Fanon, the visceral indictment, and a range of other possibilities and cedes to, valorizes, Heidegger? How does Heidegger gain ascendancy? How does he gain this primacy of voice that is also, it is critical to recognize, politically effective? How does (my) thinking lead so appropriately to Heidegger? And here it is necessary to admit that the choices delineated just now were not operative in that moment of thinking. I did not, of this I am sure, "choose" Heidegger over Malcolm X. I went directly to Heidegger. In thinking about what thinking wrought, I have been made to think not only about how that thought came to me but also about why it is that that thought and not any other was voiced. Found its voice in me. Made me its voice, gave me precisely the voice I needed.

Saliently, then, thinking is not only what the voice permits audibility. Ergo: thinking is not only about what the voice articulates, is "allowed" to say, but what the voice knows it must not say. The voice as Ego, not Id: the voice as that instrument of thinking that makes of thinking nothing less than the first question of thinking—thinking about how I came think this. How proximate to thinking is the voice?

The voice, then, is the foremost instrument of disruption in two ways. The voice, my voice—"If you can match my Cornell faculty salary"—disrupts the line of inquiry the white woman intended to pursue. In this regard, the voice erupts out of me: it explodes, if only for a moment, a small moment in a small U.S. college town, a racist stereotype; it performs a kind of disciplined rhetorical act against which the white woman—and the man—can never be immunized. The white couple in the white Volvo had no option but to do what they did: drive away. The voice articulated, brought vividly to life, the presence in the woman's question of a patronizing, class-based racism. The disruptive order of the Other's voice brought the presence of a reprehensible but resilient politics into the worst possible light. The presence of the thing is never more palpable and powerful than when it speaks itself without having to be voiced. The thing, moreover, voiced in the conditional that contains within it, if not a threat, then an unmistakable challenge: "Only," "Only if," to begin the sentence contingently, to begin the sentence, almost, appropriately, in medias res. (This *Gesprach*, about race and racism in America, it has been going on for a very long time; the Cayuga Heights encounter is but one more instance of it.) In other words, audible in the conditional opening is something more than the challenge, Are you up to this? It is more even than the outright—aggressive—throwing down of the philosophical gauntlet: not only "Can you match my Cornell faculty salary?" but can you match my thinking? How is it you have been thinking about race? How is it you have not had to think about race? That is the question that is answered negatively, because that is not the work of thinking that the woman has undertaken, that she has ever needed to undertake—to think; she certainly has no aptitude for or concept of the Derridean "injunction."

The sentence could begin, as it properly needed to, in medias res because it hinged on something in addition to the moment of its articulation. The conditional "Only" marks the history of that sentence, my reaching back—long before I knew it even as I was doing it—to the unmarkable moment of its inception. Only the sentence, only the voice that gave the sentence life, could point to the first stirrings, the first thinking, of the sentence that began with "Only." Every sentence, we can be sure, has its own history. More importantly, every sentence knows its own history.

The UnExceptional

A SISYPHEAN MOMENT for the black man as the taillights of the white Volvo disappear up the hill. I did not turn to follow those lights as the couple disappeared up the hill along Remington Road to who knows where. Clearly, however, those lights have not disappeared. They can still be seen, if only in outline; they can be glimpsed in the suppressed tremors of my disrupted thinking, of the thinking they have demanded of my Unthought. The order of the voices, the woman's, mine, the silent voice of the man in the passenger's seat, has erupted and taken up residence in my thinking. I know, for an absolute fact, that I am not the only black man or woman possessed of a PhD or some equivalent qualification who has been addressed in such a fashion, confronted with such a question, by a white person. My Cayuga Heights encounter has its equivalent, as I have already suggested, in the Latino professor in Texas or California mowing his lawn and being assaulted with a very similar—perhaps more aggressive, perhaps more polite—version of "Would you like another job?"

Mine is an unexceptional encounter: it is at once a routine occurrence for black people in American life, rendering it unexceptional, and also distinct because of my answer (what it did to me, what Heidegger did for me, etc.) and because of how it provoked me into thinking Heidegger and race and, of course, because of the oddness—the contaminatedness, the singularity—with which this coupling produced me in the demand for its voicing. As a result, Guy Fawkes Day 2013 makes of mine an unexceptional encounter. And because of the encounter, a range of voices, some of whom I cannot even hear, some of whom I will never hear, have taken up residence in my thinking about what it is my thinking effected on Guy Fawkes Day 2013.

The question of thinking assumes, only superficially, proper names: "Heidegger," "Malcolm X," "Du Bois," "Fanon." These names derive their effects from their uncanny, but obvious, capacity to mark itineraries of thought, political genealogies. How is it that Heidegger, and Heidegger alone, can provide the thinking requisite, entirely appropriate, to the moment? The answer is shockingly simple and can be located without reservation in *Was heißt Denken?* The Heideggerian effect is such that it makes the expletive no longer explicable or necessary. The Heideggerian effect makes the expletive, or the understandable impulse to name the thing that is so perceptibly present, redundant. Malcolm X and Fanon and the expletive can only return in the form of the Unthought—they can be traced to my thinking, there are traces of them in my thinking from the very beginning. And yet they can be discerned, but only discerned, to phrase this hyperbolically, as a superfluity.

I cannot, in reflecting upon that encounter, imagine a more forceful, or contradictory, endorsement of thinking than that. To think about race while giving up an archive of anti-racist thought because that archive is not proper, or necessary, to that moment. The joke is on the white woman, on me, on Heidegger, all at the same time, all because of this one encounter. Lacan, Hegel, *Aufhebung*.

How fitting, how appropriate, then, the time of the Cayuga Heights encounter. Guy Fawkes Day 2013 marks my irruption into thinking: the explosion of a canon of thought (against racism, colonialism); the massively provocative intellectual effects that thinking has on any essentialist mode of being. Thinking is impatient with any kind of identity politics, with any archive that proscribes. The institution of thinking must, just as that seventeenth-century radical intended to do to the British Parliament with the Gunpowder Plot, be true to itself only if it is willing to, time and time again, blow itself up. Thinking demands fidelity to thinking and thinking only. All the demands that thinking makes come from thinking, are intended to advance thinking (to answer, in Heidegger's terms, the question, What is called thinking? [*Was heißt Denken?*]), because without thinking as thinking, there can be no "Only if you can match my Cornell faculty salary." Again, only Heidegger, and Heidegger alone, could have given me that. He gave me that after he demanded that I think about (nothing but) thinking.

In this regard, maybe we should posit Guy Fawkes Day only secondarily as an incendiary event, as an explosion into the antidemocratic politics of seventeenth-century Britain. Maybe we should approach Guy Fawkes Day as the occasion for an insight that is routine in its philosophical expectation—routine by Heidegger's standards, anyway—but explosive in its effects: Guy Fawkes Day comes to us as a kind of political and philosophical epiphany when we least expect it. One moment you're raking leaves, the next you're thanking Martin Heidegger. The truth is, we should just always be prepared to hear things explode, we should always be prepared to think (and thank) the Unthought, we should try, as far as possible, to anticipate the irruption of the untimely thinker into our midst, and we should always be ready to voice our own unexceptionality. As long, of course, as we are more prepared than ever on Guy Fawkes Day to hear the political (race) explosion and intellectual implosion (all canons of thought are susceptible to thinking) that thinking can set off. However, what is most revealing about the paradox that thinking provokes is whom it compels you to thank. You never know which thinker is going to save your life.

Acknowledgments

I thank David Faflik, David Ellison, Jernej Habjan, and Jeff Nealon for their readings of the manuscript. It would have been considerably poorer without their insights. To Bogdan Stefanescu (Bucharest), Mladen Dolar (Ljubljana), and Dirk Uffelmann (Passau): thanks for exposing me to audiences who presented new challenges.

Special thanks are due to my editor, Danielle Kasprzak, who recognized what mattered from the first; to Anne Carter, for her splendid support; and to the insightfulness of my reader, Dana Nelson. Thanks to Ms. Sharon Powers for being a wonderful librarian.

As always, I am indebted to Juanita. She read the manuscript despite her dislike for Heidegger. *Gracias, mi amor.* For Nip, who, by turns, enthralls and exasperates—I love you; for Alex, who writes; and for Bug, who continues to amaze with her love.

Finally, to my brother Glynn: I think of you, often.

April 2015
Ithaca, New York

Grant Farred teaches at Cornell University. His most recent book is *In Motion, At Rest: The Event of the Athletic Body* (University of Minnesota Press, 2014); his previous works include *What's My Name? Black Vernacular Intellectuals* (University of Minnesota Press, 2003), *Long Distance Love: A Passion for Football* (2008), and *Phantom Calls: Race and the Globalization of the NBA* (2006).